1200 FUN, RANDOM, AND INTERESTING FACTS TO WIN TRIVIA

SCOTT MATTHEWS

7 BENEFITS OF READING FACTS

1. Knowledge
2. Stress Reduction
3. Mental Stimulation
4. Better Writing Skills
5. Vocabulary Expansion
6. Memory Improvement
7. Stronger Analytical Thinking Skills

The more that you read, the more things you will know. The more you learn, the more places you'll go.

— Dr. Seuss

ABOUT THE AUTHOR

Scott Matthews is a geologist, world traveller and author of the 'Amazing World Facts' series! He was born in Brooklyn New York by immigrant parents from the Ukraine but grew up in North Carolina. Scott studied at Duke University where he graduated with a degree in Geology and History.

His studies allowed him to travel the globe where he saw and learned amazing trivial knowledge with his many encounters. With the vast amount of interesting information he accumulated he created his best selling books 'Random, Interesting & Fun Facts You Need To Know'.

He hopes these facts will provide you with hours of fun, knowledge, entertainment and laughter.

★ ★ ★ ★ ★

If you gain any knowledge from this book, think it's fun and could put a smile on someone's face, he would greatly appreciate your review on Amazon.

1200 FACTS

1. The happier a cow, the more milk it produces. Just calling cows by individual names increases production by 3.5%.
2. Microlattice is a new type of metal created by Boeing that is 99.99% air. It is so light that it can actually sit on top of a dandelion without crushing it.
3. Every time an event is recalled by your brain, it distorts it just a little bit. In fact, when you remember something that happened in the past, you're actually remembering the last time that you remembered it, and so on.
4. Due to having such little mass, ants can't be injured from impact no matter how high a height they're dropped from.
5. Sea otters have skin pockets. There they keep their favorite rocks which they use for cracking open mollusks and clams.
6. According to research conducted by scientists, self-discipline is a better indicator of success than your IQ score.
7. The only bird with a bill longer than its body is the sword-billed hummingbird.
8. The monkey in "Hangover 2" is the same one seen in "Night at the Museum." His name is Crystal and he's featured in twenty five other movies as well. He was awarded the Poscar in 2015, which is an Oscar for animals.

9. The most armed country in the world is the US with almost ninety guns per one hundred people.
10. There are more neurons lining your stomach than there are in your spinal cord, so basically the digestive system can work without depending on the brain. That is why when you are flooded with emotion, the neurons react and you get a gut feeling.
11. Archaeologists discovered the bones of a crocodile in 2009 that could gallop. They lived approximately one hundred million years ago along with the dinosaurs, sometimes even eating them.
12. Mexican drug cartels made half a trillion dollars in 2019. To put things into perspective that's more than what Walmart earned.
13. In the patent for toilet paper, inventor Seth Wheeler made a drawing showing that toilet paper should go over, not under.
14. There is a marine park in Japan that has little holes in the otter enclosure so that visitors can shake their hands.
15. In Sweden, blood donors are notified via text message whenever their blood helps save a life.
16. The last man to be executed in the US by a firing squad was James W. Rogers. The last request from him was a bulletproof vest.
17. The reason why there are holes at the top of pen caps is to prevent you from choking if swallowed.
18. A student in 1979 could pay off their college tuition by working 385 hours, however, a student now would have to work over 7,000 hours to do the same.
19. The way Google maps shows that there is a traffic jam is by how many android phones are in that area.
20. In order to reduce cases of dengue fever and other diseases, Scientists from Florida State in the US are planning to release genetically modified mosquitoes into the wild. The males still mate with females, but the hatchlings die before adulthood due to the presence of new genes.
21. In November, 2016, the world's heaviest earthworm was found in the vegetable garden of a man named Paul Rees in Cheshire

County, England. It was named Dave; it measured almost sixteen inches (forty centimeters) long and weighed nearly twenty nine grams, which is almost twice as heavy as any other earthworm ever found.

22. In northeast Illinois the oldest octopus fossil was discovered which dates back approximately 296 million years.
23. According to the Endangered Species Act of 1973, as of 2016, 1,367 species of animals and 901 species of plants were listed as endangered or threatened.
24. Steve Jobs, the creator of Apple, didn't want his own kids to have iPads and even limited their use of technology to a minimum.
25. A Stanford study revealed that there is a high correlation between walking and creative thought output in comparison to sitting. Results showed that those who walked demonstrated a 60% increase in creative thought output.
26. Our urge to breathe mainly comes from our bodies wanting to get rid of carbon dioxide, not because of our need for oxygen.
27. There is a worldwide mega-colony of Argentinian ants. In fact, if they traveled to a different continent, they would actually be welcomed by a foreign branch of the colony.
28. On June 17, 2007, the Czech TV weather report was hacked by an art collective known for pulling off elaborate pranks. The group replaced the weather image with a live nuclear blast complete with mushroom cloud, giving the illusion that there was an actual nuclear bomb going off right there at that moment live.
29. According to research done by the University of Toronto, people who trust more are better at spotting liars.
30. The cicada killer wasp is a type of wasp that paralyzes cicadas with its venom and takes it to a burrow. There the wasp lays an egg under its left or right second leg; then when the egg hatches, the larvae eat the cicada, but carefully to still keep it alive.
31. Hawks have up to one million photoreceptors in the retina, so their vision is about eight times more accurate than humans, who only have 200,000 photoreceptors.

32. One of the very first soup kitchens was actually started by gangster Al Capone in Chicago, back in 1931.
33. Shark teeth are coated with fluoride. It acts like toothpaste keeping the shark's mouth healthy and clean.
34. A "Bass Pro Shops" mega store located in Memphis, Tennessee, is the sixth-tallest pyramid in the world.
35. In 2001, a lion cub, bear cub, and tiger cub were found abandoned in a drug dealer's basement. They were soon adopted by a sanctuary and have lived together ever since, showing a strong friendship among them.
36. Instead of floating to the top, the bubbles in Guinness beer actually sink to the bottom.
37. The world's largest treehouse was built by Minister Horace Burgess outside of Crossville, Tennessee. A still-living white oak tree eighty foot (twenty four meter) tall with a 12.1 foot (3.7 meter) diameter base supports the almost ninety eight foot (thirty meter) tall treehouse and church, while six other oak trees provide additional support.
38. While digging in a mine two miles (3.2 kilometers) below the Earth's surface, researchers have discovered the oldest known pool of water on the planet in Ontario, Canada. It's estimated that the water has been there for almost two billion years.
39. The little brown myotis bat can consume up to a thousand mosquitoes in one hour.
40. In 1927, American aviator Charles Augustus Lindbergh made the first solo nonstop flight across the Atlantic. The pilot was a polygamist with three other families and wives in Germany and Switzerland.
41. In March of 2017, in commemoration of artist David Bowie, a set of royal stamps became available for people in Britain to use. He is actually the first single artist to have this honor.
42. In Denmark, if you buy a new car, you have to pay a registration tax on the new vehicle of 150%. The tax was actually reduced by the Danish government from 180%. This was all part of its 2016 budget.
43. A set of identical twins separated at birth went on to live similarly eerily lives. Both boys were named James but went by

the name Jim. They both had a childhood dog named Toy. They both married twice, first to a woman named Linda and then to a woman named Betty. They both had sons named James Alan, both were sheriffs in separate Ohio counties, and both drove Chevrolets.

44. In 2014, a study done by the Stanford School of Medicine showed that the blood of young mice has the ability to restore the mental capacities in old mice. When given infusions of blood plasmas from young mice to old mice, old mice actually outperformed on spatial memory tests, compared to those old mice that were given plasma from other old mice.

45. A pastrami-flavored pilsner was created by Shmaltz Brewing in collaboration with Barcade. It's a beer made with authentic pastrami notes, including ingredients like a pinch of kosher salt, a dash of pepper, and smoke.

46. The odds of an average golfer getting a hole in one on a par three are approximately 12,500 to one.

47. During the Second World War, the Nazis had planned to kill Sir Winston Churchill with a bar of exploding chocolate. The explosive device was coated with a thin layer of dark chocolate by Hitler's bomb makers and it was packaged in an expensive-looking black and gold paper. Fortunately, British spies discovered the plan.

48. The killer clown was the nickname given to serial killer John Wayne Gacy, who killed thirty three boys and young men in the 1970's. He used to perform as someone called "Pogo the Clown" at children's events. In fact, while being in prison, he painted several self-portraits of himself as a clown, and although most were destroyed, some still exist and are highly prized.

49. In 1989, three daycare centers were forced to remove their murals of Mickey, Donald, and Goofy, under threat of legal action by Disney.

50. American company Cabot Guns has manufactured the first gun made almost entirely from a piece of Gibeon meteorite. The meteorite was originally found in Namibia in the 1830's and it crashed on Earth about 4.5 billion years ago.

51. Bill Gates used to be so addicted to Minesweeper that he actually had to uninstall it on his own computer because he was playing it too much.
52. Joe Munch was given the shortest jail sentence in history of only one minute in jail. His crime was being drunk and disorderly but the judge didn't want to punish him, just "teach him a lesson."
53. If you search the number 241543903 on Google images, you get a bunch of pictures of people sticking their heads in a freezer.
54. An ultracrepidarians is a person who always gives their opinion and thoughts on topics they have little expertise in.
55. In 1964, in Hamilton, Ontario, the first Tim Hortons Donut Shop opened. Coffee and doughnuts would cost only ten cents each. The apple fritter and the dutchie are two of the original doughnuts that were offered from its opening.
56. In 1990, a man named Jesse Sharp paddled over the Niagara Falls in a kayak. His plan was to paddle on after the fall to a restaurant downstream where he had made restaurant reservations. Jesse didn't wear a life jacket and his body was never found.
57. In 2013, in order to help tackle the problem of alcoholism in the country, scientists from the University of Chile developed a new vaccine that will give anyone who drinks even a small amount of alcohol an immediate, very bad hangover.
58. In 1987, to commemorate a visit by Pope John Paul II, the Hollywood sign was changed to Holywood. The prank, however, was undone before the pope arrived in LA.
59. In some countries such as Britain, Ireland, Norway, Iceland, and New Zealand, police officers are unarmed when they are on patrol. In fact, they are only equipped with guns under special situations. This is rooted in the belief that arming the police with guns causes more violence than it prevents.
60. The only mammals that don't pee or poo during the winter hibernation months are bears. In fact, doctors have studied how the bears recycle their urine to help human patients with kidney failure.

61. There is an algae that tastes like bacon when fried which has nearly twice the nutritional value as kale. The algae was developed by scientists at Oregon State University.
62. There is a 1966 Volvo with more than three million miles (4,800,000 kilometers) on it. The average lifetime of a car is 150,000 miles (240,000 kilometers).
63. In the 18th century, in the Gregorian period, little beauty patches known as mouches were used by women to cover blemishes, like smallpox scars. They would often use small clippings of black velvet, silk, or satin; but those who couldn't afford silk or satin had to use a piece of mouse skin.
64. Arcuate is the name given to the orange stitching on the back pockets of Levi jeans. It has literally no function and during World War II, it was painted on as rationing.
65. Wales holds a world mountain bike bog snorkeling championship. Contenders have to ride a mountain bike as fast as they can along the bottom of a bog, which has a 6.5 feet (two meter) deep, water-filled trench. To make it more difficult, the bikes that they use have led-filled frames, the tires are filled with water, and the competitors wear led weight belts so that they don't float off of their bikes.
66. India had a successful mission to Mars in 2014 that cost less than the movie "Gravity", that starred George Clooney and Sandra Bullock. The Mars mission cost fifty eight million dollars (USD) while the movie cost seventy five million dollars (USD).
67. The tooth fairy is actually a mouse in France. It's known as the "la bon petite souris" and it will take the teeth left under pillows replacing them with cash or sweets.
68. Canada declared war on Japan after Pearl Harbor, the first western nation that did so. The US declared war the day after.
69. A wholphin is a cross between a false killer whale and a bottlenose dolphin.
70. The rights of some of the Stephen King's short stories are sold by the author for just one dollar. He refers to them as his "dollar babies" and he sells them so that film students can use them to make movies.

71. The Yakuza is known as Japan's largest organized crime syndicate. During both the 1995 and 2001 Japanese earthquakes, they provided food, water, blankets, diapers, and other supplies to those in need. They even had a faster response time than the Japanese government.
72. The first US president to be born in a hospital was President Jimmy Carter.
73. There are some types of fireworks that can be set off in daylight by using colored smoke.
74. Up until 2013, drug trafficking in Singapore was punished with a mandatory death sentence. As far as harsh drug laws are concerned, Singapore had and still has some of the toughest out of any country in the world.
75. The Heart Attack Grill is a restaurant in Las Vegas that offers the burger with the most calories in the world. According to Jon Basso, the owner, the Octuple Bypass Burger is 20,000 calories. The restaurant ended up making national headlines for killing its customers.
76. "Aquaman crystals" are a type of crystals created by scientists at the University of South Denmark that can absorb a roomful of oxygen and store it for later use. This invention could actually be the key to underwater breathing. A handful of crystals could pull oxygen from the water and provide divers with air.
77. When actress Sissy Spacek played the role of a teenager in the movie Carrie, she was actually twenty six years old. The movie was based on Stephen King's first novel.
78. If you chew gum for eighteen hours, apply lip balm 1,500 times, or sing a song twenty three times, you would burn off 200 calories.
79. We can train our brain to slow down time by observing and paying attention to things more closely. This is due to the fact that when memories are created with more detail, moments seem to last longer and the brain takes longer to note down this information, making time seem like it's moving slower.
80. The "Super STEM 3" is a super powered electron microscope

that can examine objects a million times smaller than a human hair.
81. When in danger or frightened, the opossum is known to play dead. It is actually an involuntary reaction, as the animal enters a comatose state as a defense mechanism. Once the fear is gone, they wake up again.
82. In the US, there is fully edible six-pack beer can packaging. It was created by the Saltwater Brewery from Florida. It's made from byproducts of the brewing process like wheat and barley, and is fully biodegradable and totally digestible. They are as strong as the plastic ones, but if an animal or bird gets caught in one, they can actually eat it and quickly decompose it.
83. During World War II, Germany used guns that had a curved barrel device that was clamped onto the end of an MP 44 rifle. The guns allowed soldiers to shoot over obstacles without exposing themselves to return fire.
84. The only official place on Earth named "Earth" is a town called Texas.
85. The Atlas moth imitates a snake's appearance and behavior in order to defend itself. It has convincing wing patterns and when threatened, it will fall to the ground and flop around to look like a writhing snake.
86. Liberia, Burma, and the United States are the only three countries in the world that don't use the metric system.
87. In Grenoble, France, there are vending machines that will print out a free, quick short story for you to read while you are on the bus or train. Depending on how much time you have to kill, it's possible to print out a one, three, or five minute story.
88. In 1890, when the Ouija Board was asked what it should be called, it spelled out "Ouija." After when it was asked what it meant, it said "Good Luck."
89. Sphygmomanometer is the device that measures blood pressure.
90. In 1857, at McGill University in Montreal, Canada, Thomas Dairy Hunt invented the green ink used in American money.
91. Interscatter is a way of communication developed by Engineers

at the University of Washington that converts Bluetooth signals into Wi-Fi signals. This way of communicating would allow contact lenses and brain implants to send signals to your iPhone.
92. The nose of a mosquito, known as proboscis, has forty seven sharp edges on its tip to help cut through skin. They can even cut through protective clothing.
93. Jump Man was originally the name of Super Mario.
94. The longest glass sky bridge in the world is in Zhangjiajie, China, which is 1,400 feet (430 meters).
95. The Shanghai Tower, known for being the world's second tallest building, built the world's fastest elevator in late 2016. According to Mitsubishi, its manufacturer, the elevator moves as fast as 4,000 feet (1,200 meters) per minute, which is forty six miles (seventy four kilometers) per hour.
96. With more than 250,000 lakes, Ontario, Canada, contains about one-fifth of the whole world's fresh water.
97. The male emperor moth is able to detect pheromones from the female emperor moth from miles away.
98. According to a study conducted by Psychological Science, only 1% of friendships made in the 7th grade remain intact by the 12th grade.
99. Some babies are born with a condition called lidling, where the top part of the cartilage in the ear is basically folded so the top ridge is kind of rounded over. It's possible to reshape their ears however, by using a mold called "Ear Well" that can change their shape in about six weeks.
100. The skunk is not the animal with the strongest of smell out there. The lesser anteater gives off a pungent odor that is about four to seven times stronger than that of a skunk. It's so strong that you can smell it up to 164 feet (fifty meters) away.
101. The most recorded song in history is "Yesterday" by The Beatles, written by Paul McCartney. More than 4,000 versions of the song have been recorded.
102. In the 1996 movie "Twister," the sound for the tornado was recorded from a camel's moan which was then slowed down.
103. In the early days of the Indie 500, having an onboard mechanic was mandatory. Cars then used to have two seats,

one for the driver and one for the onboard mechanic. The mechanic monitored the gauges, made repairs, and sometimes would even massage the driver's arms and neck. The onboard mechanic was mandatory from 1912 to 1922, and then again from 1930 to 1937.
104. "Eureka, I have found it" is California's state motto. It refers to the discovery of God and it appears on the state seal.
105. Until 1992, electrical appliances were often sold in Britain without plugs on the end of them and consumers had to attach them themselves.
106. The only letter in the alphabet that doesn't appear in any US territory or state name is the letter "Q."
107. In Southeast Asia, around sixty million people rely on the Mekong River Base for food. In fact, the river is home to more giant fish than any other river on Earth.
108. About 25% to 40% of people have motion sickness, a sensation of dizziness that occurs when you are on a car, boat, plane, or train. According to the University of Maryland Medical Center, women are more susceptible than men and Asians are more susceptible than white or black people.
109. China celebrates over ten million weddings every year. With couples spending an average of $12,000 on each wedding that's a total of $120 billion.
110. Soldiers during the first world war would fire hundreds of random shots over their trenches to boil the coolant water in their machine guns, just so they could make some tea.
111. In 1871, Mark Twain invented and received a patent for the elastic clasp bra strap under his original name, Samuel Clemens. His patent said: "The nature of my invention consists in an adjustable and detachable elastic trap for vests, pantaloons or other garments requiring straps as will hereinafter more fully set forth."
112. The brain does not have any pain receptors, so if you were having brain surgery, you wouldn't feel any pain.
113. There are plans in Berlin to create a building called 'The House of One" which welcomes Jews, Christians, and Muslims, all under one roof where they can worship their gods together.

114. The role of Gandalf in the Lord of the Rings trilogy was offered to actor Sean Connery, in exchange of $10 million and 15% of box office takings for all three movies. The actor, however, rejected the offer because he didn't understand the script.
115. Between 2010 and 2015, the population in China actually shrunk by one million people.
116. The strongest winds in our solar system occur on the planet Neptune, with winds up to 1,304 miles (2,100 kilometers) an hour. To put that into perspective, hurricane winds on Earth run at speeds of up to only 191 miles (119 kilometers) an hour.
117. The metabolism of hummingbirds is so high that they are always hours away from starving to death.
118. Approximately 3.1 billion people a year are transported by the Tokyo subway system.
119. In the United States, when someone reports their company for tax evasion, the person receives anywhere from 15-30% of the amount collected. A man named Bradley Birkenfeld was a whistleblower on the USB AG Swiss Bank tax evasion scheme and received $104 million as a reward.
120. Bald eagles build nests that are usually about five feet (1.5 meters) in diameter. The same nests are normally used year after year and they can become even bigger, as big as nine feet (2.7 meters), and weigh as much as two tons.
121. There is a famous Mosque in Iran known as "Nasir Almoque Mosque" for its amazing stained glass windows. When the sun shines through them during the day, the inside of the mosque looks like a kaleidoscope.
122. Smells can influence our dreams according to a study done in 2008. Subjects of the study were exposed to the scent of roses while sleeping, giving nearly all of them pleasant dreams. However, when the air around those subjects was infused with the smell of rotten eggs while sleeping, they had negative dreams.
123. To reduce delivery damages, Dutch bike manufacturer VanMoof started printing pictures of flat screen TV's on their bike boxes. Damages went down 70 to 80%.

124. Stephen Hawking's son, Tim Hawking, once added swear words to his dad's voice synthesizer as a prank.
125. Fourteen year old teenager Al Capone was expelled from school for hitting a female teacher and he never went back.
126. If you were recruited during the American Civil War, you could pay someone $300 to go in your place. This was called commutation and it was intended to raise money for the war effort. However, it was often deeply criticized as it was better at raising money than troops.
127. On March 27, 1977, one of the deadliest air plane crashes of all time happened on the ground. When KLM Royal Dutch Airline Boeing 747 started to take off, it crashed into a Pan American World Airways Boeing 747 that was still on the airstrip. The tragedy occurred at the Los Rodeos Airport in the Canary Islands, killing a total of 574 people from both planes.
128. An SPF 30 sunscreen that smells like fried chicken was released by KFC, in August of 2016. It went out to promote their extra crispy recipe.
129. The only countries to have both Mediterranean and Atlantic coastlines are Morocco, France, and Spain.
130. Gordon Matthew Thomas Sumner is actually the real name of musician and singer Sting. The nickname Sting was given by band leader Gordon Solomon of the Phoenix Jazzmen because he would perform on stage in a sweater that made him look like a giant bee.
131. Years ago, snakes could actually slither and walk because they used to have legs. Eventually, they evolved into legless creatures, although the gene to grow limbs still exists.
132. Richard Feynman, a famous American physicist, was named the world's smartest man by Omni Magazine. His mother was actually quoted as saying: "If that's the world's smartest man, God help us."
133. In Canada, lawn darts with pointy, elongated tips are banned.
134. Naturally blond people represent only 2% of the entire world's population.
135. In Japan, the Japanese Anniversary Association officially

recognized May 9 as Goku Day. In Japanese the number five is pronounced "go" and the number nine is pronounced "ku."

136. The Statue of Liberty was packed in 214 crates containing 350 pieces when it was shipped from France to New York.

137. When he was a teenager, actor Tom Cruise was a student at a Franciscan seminary. In fact, he aspired to become a priest before he went into acting.

138. Based on a study performed by the sociologist Nick Wolfinger at the University of Utah, people have a better chance of not getting divorced if they get married between the ages of twenty eight and thirty two.

139. It's estimated that 350 million people worldwide suffer from depression according to the World Health Organization. This disorder is also a primary cause of disability in the world and is a major contributor to the overall global burden of disease.

140. Abraham Lincoln, the 16th president of the United States, never actually slept in the Lincoln bedroom. He would rather use it as his personal office.

141. Based on research done at Norway's University of Bergen, there is a link between being addicted to work and anxiety. They studied more than 16,000 workers across the country and found that almost 8% of workaholics were more likely to suffer from ADHD, OCD, depression, and anxiety. The study also revealed that people who work more than fifty five hours per week were at a higher risk of heart attacks and strokes.

142. April 14 is known as Black Day in Korea. On this day, single people who didn't receive anything for Valentine's Day or "White Day" get together dressed in black and eat black noodles together.

143. The temperature of milk that has just been freshly milked from a cow is 100 degrees Fahrenheit (37.8 degrees Celsius).

144. The Rungrado May Day Stadium is the biggest stadium in the world. It's located in Pyongyang, North Korea, and it was completed on May 1, 1989. Although it houses different sporting events, it is more famous for being the place where the annual Mass Games are held, an artistic and gymnastic event with over 100,000 participants in it.

145. According to different studies, people who stay up late, known also as night owls, tend to be more extravagant, impulsive, and novelty seeking. They are also more likely to develop addictive behaviors, mental disorders, and antisocial tendencies.
146. In Japan, there are special retirement homes for senior dogs. There, they get the proper care and love they need for their last years of life.
147. Picasso was once asked "Did you do this?" of his painting "Guernica", a painting of German bombings on the town of Guernica, by a German officer. His response was: "No, you did."
148. In the town of Hakone, in the southeastern part of Japan, there is a spa called "Yunessun Spa House" that offers ramen noodle baths. The bath consists of ramen pork broth and synthetic noodles. It allegedly helps improve a patient's skin.
149. The US penny used to be composed of 95% copper and 5% zinc before World War II. But because those metals were unavailable during the war, they were then made of zinc coated steel. The final change was made in 1982, after several revisions to the composition, to 97.6% zinc and 2.4% copper, and is still used today.
150. President Thomas Jefferson was fluent in English, Greek, Latin, French, German, and Spanish. He also studied Arabic, Gaelic, and Welsh. He remains the most multilingual president of the United States in history.
151. As the result of people doing the ice bucket challenge, the ALS Association received $101 million in donations. That was a huge amount compared to the $2.8 million raised the previous year.
152. Harry Truman, the 33rd President of the United States, and Gerald Ford, the 38th President, both died on the same date, December 26.
153. Most eyes on predators are facing forward while most eyes on prey are on the sides of their head.
154. Approximately 80% of YouTube views occur outside the United States. In fact, YouTube exists in over eighty eight

countries, under seventy six different languages, which covers about 95% of the Internet's population.
155. Disney World is sixty nine square miles (111 square kilometers). That is about the same size as the city of San Francisco and twice the size of Manhattan.
156. If you add cold cream to your coffee, it actually keeps it warmer longer, compared to just having black coffee.
157. In Sri Lanka, elephants are sacred animals. In fact, they are protected under the Sri Lankan law and killing one carries the death penalty.
158. Phytophotodermatitis, also known as margarita dermatitis or lime disease (not to be confused with Lyme disease with a Y), is a toxic reaction that results from citric acid mixed with sunlight. It can cause second degree burns and is very painful.
159. Based on a study led by zoologist Igor Malyshev, at St. Petersburg State University in Russia, the Australian red kangaroo and the eastern gray kangaroo are almost always left-handed.
160. Dr. James Naismith from Almonte, Canada, is actually the inventor of the basketball game. Back in 1891, he cut out the bottom of a peach basket and hung it ten feet (three meters) in the air, and thus the game was born.
161. Carmine is a type of food coloring extracted from female cochineal insect shells boiled in ammonia or sodium carbonate solution. It is actually used in more things than you might think, like ice cream, yogurt, candy, and red fruit drinks.
162. Kawaii is a cooking trend in Japan. It's a form of miniature cooking where people create mini edible cuisine using little stoves, pots, pans, and cooking utensils, as well as real-life ingredients that are cooked over a candle flame.
163. The beelzebufo ampinga, known also as the devil frog, may be the largest frog that ever existed according to National Geographic. These beach ball sized amphibians that are now extinct, grew to almost 1.67 feet (half a meter) long and weighed approximately ten pounds (4.5 kilograms).
164. It's possible to buy a 4K motion activated Wi-Fi camera for your bird feeder called "Bird Photo Booth." The device allows

you to take close-up pictures and videos of the birds that drop in for a meal.

165. There are some marine bird species, like the penguin, that have a supraorbital gland placed just above their eyes which can remove sodium chloride from their blood stream. The gland works just like our kidneys, removing salt, and allowing penguins to survive when they have no access to fresh water. The penguin excretes the salt byproduct as brine through its bill.

166. Sam Griner, from the "Successful Kid Memes" group, used his fame to start a GoFundMe page. The site raised nearly $100,000 for his dad's kidney transplant.

167. During the opening ceremony of the Olympic Games, the procession is always led by the Greek team. Then all other teams follow in alphabetical order with the exception of the last team to enter, which is the team that is hosting the event.

168. US Senator Gaylord Nelson actually founded "Earth Day" as a way to promote the environmental movement. On April 22, 1970, the first-ever "Earth Day" was held. It has been celebrated on that day every year since.

169. Fireflies are actually beetles, not flies as we may think. Most of them are winged and belong to the same family as the glow worm.

170. While filming Disney's Napoleon and Samantha, eight year old actress Jodie Foster was attacked by a lion and briefly carried in its mouth. She has had a fear of cats ever since.

171. After the winter ice melts, Lake Michigan in Traverse City becomes so clear that you are able to see shipwrecks 298 feet (91 meters) below the water.

172. A man named Julien Barreaux from France spent several months finding the online character who stabbed him on an online game. He found the person living just a few miles away, and when he saw him in real life, stabbed him in the chest.

173. Adult coloring books are becoming a huge trend and publishers actually struggle to keep up with demand. The books seem to be a way to successfully reduce stress and relieve anxiety. They

are even used as rehabilitation aids for patients who are recovering from strokes.
174. Before Martin Luther King Jr. went up to do his famous speech in Washington in 1963, he added the "I have a dream" line minutes before he started.
175. Duke, a nine year old Great Pyrenees dog, is the honorary mayor of Cormorant Township, in Minnesota. He is actually in his third term.
176. In Saudi Arabia, movie theaters are completely forbidden. They were banned in the 1980's.
177. Markus Notch Persson created the first version of the popular video game Minecraft in just six days, originally calling it "cave game". To date the game has sold over 144 million copies.
178. There are thousands of rogue planets in the universe and it's plausible that many of these could actually hold life.
179. The Skunklock is a bike lock developed by US entrepreneur Daniel Idzkowski and Swiss-born engineer Yves Perrenoud. When cut by a potential thief, the lock emits a noxious chemical that induces vomiting and makes it hard to see or breath.
180. Coffee beans are not beans, they are actually fruit pits.
181. It's estimated that every three days, the equivalent of the world's population use Otis elevators, escalators, and walkways.
182. In 1874, a fifteen year old boy named Chester Greenwood from Maine invented the earmuffs. He shaped two pieces of wire into circles and then connected them with a wire headband. To keep out the wind, his grandmother sewed velvet and beaver fur to the circles. In 1877, when he was eighteen, he got the patent, and by 1883, his factory was producing 30,000 ear muffs a year. By the time of his death in 1937, he was producing nearly half a million a year.
183. In August, 2016, a single lightning strike killed 323 reindeer in the Hardangervidda National Park, in Norway. Due to a heavy storm, they were huddled together and were killed because of ground current that had stopped all of their hearts.
184. The fear of your mother-in-law is called pentheraphobia. The

origin of the word penthera is Greek, which means mother-in-law, and phobia meaning fear.
185. A study done by The University of New South Wales found that having good manners makes people see you as a person with greater interpersonal warmth. It also makes you a happier person.
186. In Houston, Texas, there is a museum called the Art Car Museum, also known as the Garage Mahal, which is filled with ornately painted, decorated vehicles. It opened in 1998 and features a bunch of different automobiles ranging from hippy vans to police cruisers.
187. The lightest plane to ever exist is the Bede BD-5 which weighed only 357 pounds (162kg).
188. The world's longest highway is in Australia which has a total length of nine thousand miles (fourteen thousand kilometers).
189. Qatar Airways allows you to travel with a falcon in the cabin with the only condition of having less than six falcons in total aboard.
190. Given that the platypus has no nipples, the milk basically oozes from their skin.
191. The city of Moscow ran out of vodka at the end of World War 2 because the Russians partied so hard.
192. Between January 25 and January 31 in 2017, a seventy year old woman named Chau Smith from Independence, Missouri, ran seven marathons in seven days on seven continents.
193. The most expensive bottle of white wine according to the Guinness World Records is the Chateau d'Yquem from 1811. It was sold by the antique wine company for $117,000 to Christian Vanneque on January 18, 2011.
194. When the Aboriginal Canadians played lacrosse, the teams had anywhere between a hundred to a thousand people while the fields were 1,500 to 9,000 feet (500 to 3,000 meters) long. Some games went for as long as three days.
195. The planet Uranus has twenty seven moons, five of them large and the rest much smaller. The five larger moons are Miranda, Ariel, Umbriel, Titania, and Oberon.
196. Each human eye can only hold 0.00024 ounces (seven

microliters) of liquid, meaning that when you cry, the drainage ducts around the eye are flooded. That's why tears roll down your face and you get a runny nose when you cry.
197. The complete loss of your sense of smell is called anosmia. Without your sense of smell, food doesn't taste the same, you can't smell perfume or the scent of a flower, and you can find yourself in a dangerous situation unknowingly.
198. From the Spongebob Squarepants movie, David Hasselhoff owns a fourteen feet (four meter) tall replica of himself.
199. To build the Taj Mahal, more than 1,000 elephants were used to transport the materials.
200. In the 1800's, the first Tuesday in November was made election day by congress in the United States to accommodate farmers and rural workers. November was the month that suited farmers best because the fall harvest was over by then, spring was planting time, and summer was when they worked the fields. Additionally, the weather in November in most of the country was still mild enough for traveling. As far as Tuesday, it was picked because most residents of rural America had to travel far to reach the voting center, so Tuesday gave them enough time to start traveling on Monday instead of Sunday, which would have interfered with church services.
201. On the planet Uranus, summer lasts forty two years long and winter another forty two years. It's Earth's tilt that gives us our seasons, but Uranus is significantly more on its side in relation to its poles, hence the length of its seasons.
202. The Bandra-Worli Sea Link is a massive eight-lane traffic bridge built in India. Every individual cable can support more than 900 tons of weight and, if put together, it could wrap around the whole circumference of the Earth.
203. Most Americans did not support the idea of a moon landing before it actually happened, as they thought the government was spending way too much money on space.
204. It's illegal to look for a moose from an airplane in Alaska.
205. On September 5, 1698, Russian Czar Peter the Great, in an attempt to impose a more Western way of living, enforced a

beard tax on all Russian men because European men were usually clean shaven. For centuries, Russian men had worn long flowing beards and a lot of men considered it a sin to shave, so it was very difficult for some to remove their beards. The tax was up to 100 rubles, which represented a small fortune in those days, and it affected mostly the upper classes. Peasants, however, were allowed to wear beards in their villages but, if they were entering the city, they had to pay a one kopek coin.

206. Dogs can suffer from tonsillitis; however, they cannot suffer from appendicitis as they don't have an appendix.
207. "Beano" was originally the name for bing. It was called this because players used beans to cover the numbered squares.
208. The World Health Organization estimates that around 50% of all medications are prescribed, dispensed, or sold inappropriately. Even more, half of the patients don't even take their medication correctly.
209. Jill Hubley, a web designer based in Brooklyn, New York, created a detailed map identifying every single tree in New York City, based on the last tree census data back in 2005.
210. The hagfish doesn't have bones in its body and has the ability to tie itself into a knot.
211. The French bulldog actually originated in England. It wasn't until English lace makers took them to France where they got their French moniker.
212. Crab claws have muscles so strong that they can produce a pinch force of up to sixty pounds (twenty seven kilograms)
213. 600,000 South Korean students sat for their highly competitive college entrance tests in November, 2016, an event that would determine their future. To ensure that all students got to school on time, business opening hours were delayed, lorries were banned from roads, and construction was stopped. During language tests which required listening, airport authorities shut down all takeoffs and landings for half an hour so the noise wouldn't affect nearby schools.
214. The tongue is the part of the human body that heals the quickest. Due to the rich supply of blood that the tongue

receives, any injury there is, is able to heal twice as fast than any other part of the body.
215. The biologists from the University of North Florida found that male dolphins have life long bromances with each other. They team up, acting as wingmen for each other, help herd fertile females and even keep other males from mating with some of them.
216. In 2015, in an effort to boost consumer confidence and spending, a program called "Fresh Start" was launched by Croatia. The program helped to wipe away debt for 60,000 low income Croatians who had been struggling to pay their bills. The state, along with firms and banks, agreed to forgive up to 60,000 kuna, or 8,830 dollars per citizen.
217. A boy named William Kamkwamba built a windmill from bicycle parts, gum trees and other scraps to power electrical appliances in his home when he was only fourteen years old.
218. In Brazil, there are mushrooms that can glow in the dark. They are part of the genius mycena, a group that includes about 500 species worldwide, although only thirty three are known to be bioluminescent.
219. According to estimations, the Mexican Drug Cartel Caballeros Templarios, or "The Knights Templar", makes around $152 million a year.
220. The fourth largest island in the world is the Republic of Madagascar, with an area of 364,000 square miles (586,000 square kilometers). The other three larger islands are Borneo, Greenland, and New Guinea.
221. In 2010, the University of Tubingen in Germany discovered that King Tut the Pharaoh was actually very frail and had bone disease and malaria. They believe this might have been due to incest.
222. The world record for the most tomatoes harvested from a single plant in one year is held by a tomato tree in Epcot's land pavilion, in Florida. It had a one year harvest of 32,000 tomatoes, which weighed a total of 1,150 pounds (522 kilograms).
223. When orbiting, Mercury gets so close to the sun that its surface

temperature can get as hot as 800 degrees Fahrenheit (427 degrees Celsius). However, given that there isn't much of an atmosphere there to keep all that heat trapped, when the night comes, temperatures substantially decrease, falling as low as -279 degrees Fahrenheit (-173 degrees Celsius).

224. A ten-pack of Juicy Fruit gum was the first product to be sold by scanning a barcode. The transaction occurred at 8:01 AM, on June 26, 1974, at a Marsh Supermarket in Troy, Ohio.

225. Engineers in Canada receive an iron ring to remind them to have humility upon graduation. The ring is given in memory of a bridge that collapsed twice due to incorrect calculations involving iron.

226. On the fortieth anniversary of his moon walk, Buzz Aldrin, the veteran Astronaut, recorded a song entitled "Rocket Experience", both to commemorate his historic feat, and to raise money for organizations that are committed to exploring space.

227. In 1881, a man named Theophilus Van Kannel invented the revolving door because he hated the idea of chivalry and opening doors for women.

228. There is a Japanese robotics company called Fanuc that can be run for thirty days without any supervision and the robots there can build fifty other robots in the course of a day.

229. There is a tradition in Denmark where those who are still single when turning twenty five are doused in cinnamon.

230. A cat named "Cookie" disappeared on a family trip when they went to the south of France in 2013. Eighteen months later Cookie returned home, dirty and a little skinny, but alive after having travelled over six hundred miles (one thousand kilometers).

231. According to research, about 40% of all twins have created their own language that only they can understand when using it.

232. A young girl named Michelle Rochon wrote a letter to President Kennedy in 1961 worrying about Santa's safety when the Soviets were testing nuclear bombs close to the North Pole. The President actually wrote back to Michelle stating that he

had spoken to Santa and that there was nothing to worry about.
233. The scent of freshly-mowed grass is actually the lawn's response to injury. Green leaf volatiles are volatile organic compounds released by plants. When they are injured, these emissions increase exponentially.
234. There was a study conducted in 2014 that linked sleep patterns with people's behavior and character traits. Those who stayed up later tended to be greater risk takers than those who woke up early.
235. In Japan, gun laws are so severe that after a police officer once killed himself with a gun, he was posthumously charged with breaking the law.
236. At the Nuremberg trials, genius level IQ test scores were achieved by several Nazi leaders.
237. Swarm boats are US Navy boats that don't require a captain. They are developed by the Office of Naval Research. They use a radar system to communicate with one another and are designed to overwhelm and confuse the enemy.
238. Almost three quarters of Japanese households use high-tech toilets which eliminate the use of toilet paper and include things such as a seat warmer, self-cleaner, and deodorant spritzer.
239. Andrej Ciesielski, an eighteen year old tourist in Egypt, was arrested after climbing the Great Pyramid of Giza and taking photos, which he shared with his thousands of followers. He started a trend which other copy cats have begun doing so they can also post to their social media as well.
240. In the late 1700's, many Europeans thought that the tomato was poisonous. In fact, it was nicknamed the "poison apple" because wealthy people were dying after eating them. However, the reason they died was because they were eaten off of pewter plates, which were high in lead content, so the combination of the lead and acid from the tomatoes caused lead poisoning. As a result, the tomato was feared in Europe for more than 200 years.

241. Honey reaches the bloodstream within twenty minutes after swallowing it.
242. Lizards are able to self-amputate their tails for protection and grow them back after a few months.
243. The "M's" in M&Ms stand for the last names of their founders: Mars and Murray. It's the same thing for the Mars bar itself, even though it wasn't originally named by its creator Frank Mars, but by his son Forrest Mars.
244. As a way to honor Jamaican sprinter Usain Bolt, he was given Berlin's twelve foot (3.6 meter) high piece of the Berlin Wall. It weighed nearly three tons.
245. In 2015, the Japanese army created a massive Star Wars sculpture for the yearly Sapporo Snow festival that was made from over three thousand tons of snow.
246. The University of Montreal did a study and found that anyone can become a good singer. It's a skill that you can develop and becomes better with practice and worsens by lack of use.
247. Former American presidents Thomas Jefferson and Jimmy Carter both used to be peanut farmers.
248. The three most common mental illnesses in the United States are depression, alcohol dependency, and social anxiety disorder.
249. The state of Wyoming produces nearly 40% of all coal production in the United States.
250. In Tasmania they have an extra day off known as Easter Tuesday. It's not celebrated anywhere else.
251. The grasshopper mouse is a type of carnivorous animal that is immune to venom, eats scorpions, and howls like a wolf to claim its territory.
252. When someone gets pregnant while already pregnant, that's referred to as superfetation. The second conception may happen within a few days or weeks after the first conception.
253. In 2014, a fan waving a flare at a Polish soccer game burst into flames when a security guard used pepper spray on him, without knowing that the substances were combustible.
254. Since 1947, after the Second World War was over, Norway has sent Britain a giant Norwegian Spruce Christmas tree every

year, as a symbol of Norwegian gratitude to the United Kingdom for preserving Norwegian liberty. Londoners gather every year in Trafalgar Square to participate in Christmas carols and to see the tree being lit.

255. The largest species of ribbon worms is the boot laced worm. They can grow up to 197 feet (sixty meters) in length, which is even longer than a blue whale.
256. The world's largest sea sponge was found 7,000 feet (2,134 meters) below the ocean surface when researchers were exploring the northwestern Hawaiian Islands aboard the Okeanos Explorer. It measured twelve feet (3.65 meters) long and seven feet (0.91 centimeters) wide.
257. The oldest message in a bottle spent 108 years, four months, and eighteen days at sea according to the Guinness World Records. The Marine Biological Association in the United Kingdom put the bottle in the sea in November, 1906, and it washed ashore on Amrum Island in Germany on April 17, 2015.
258. In 1948, the dispenser was invented to resemble a cigarette lighter. Its purpose was to encourage people to quit smoking.
259. In 2015, a study published in the Journal of Analytical Chemistry by a university in Albany demonstrated that gender can be determined from the concentration of amino acids that are found in a fingerprint. As it turns out, women have more amino acids than men.
260. Keisuke Yamada is a Japanese artist who creates incredible carvings out of bananas using only a spoon and a toothpick.
261. It's estimated that people throw away nearly $4.5 million into fountains and wishing wells every single year.
262. A hungry sea lion pup once walked into a fancy restaurant in San Diego, California, and sat down at a prime table with an ocean view.
263. There is a breed of cat in Turkey known as the "Van Cats" that are pure white in color, have different colored eyes and love the water.
264. Hedy Lamarr was a famous actress in the 1930's who was also a mathematician and inventor, creating a frequency hopping

spectrum technology that's currently still used in Wi-Fi and Bluetooth today.
265. If we had the same vision as an eagle, we would be able to see an ant walking on the ground from the top of a ten story building.
266. D-day was originally set for June fifth, but due to bad weather, it had to be postponed by twenty four hours.
267. Japanese Company Dentsu requests all new employees and recently promoted executives to climb Mount Fuji. The event has occured every July, since 1925.
268. Irish pirates captured St. Patrick when he was only sixteen years old and later sold him into slavery, where he was held in captivity for six years. During that time, he became deeply devoted to Christianity through constant prayer, and he actually considered his enslavement as God's test of his faith.
269. Drinking too much water can be just as harmful to your health as not drinking enough water. It is known as overhydration and it can cause nausea and vomiting, headaches, and changes in your mental state, such as confusion or disorientation.
270. In Buxton, England, a poisonous lagoon at the quarry was dyed black intentionally for safety reasons. The previous lagoon had an azure blue water color so beautiful and inviting, that the warning signs did not keep swimmers out.
271. In Wood Buffalo National Park in northern Alberta, Canada, there is a beaver dam so large that it can be seen from outer space. It spans 2,789 feet (850 meters) across.
272. Since the first nuclear test explosion on July 16, 1945, at least 2,054 nuclear test explosions have been performed by eight nations at dozens of test sites around the world.
273. Genuphobia is the fear of knees. This rare phobia is apparently common in people that have experienced traumatic knee injuries.
274. In Hong Kong, you can have a "McWedding" and for $1,200 you can get food, drinks and apple pies for fifty people.
275. The first documented case of twin dogs were born via C-section in August, 2016, at Rant en Dal Animal Hospital in Mogale City, South Africa.

276. The Redhorse Osaka Wheel in Japan is a 404 feet (123 meter) Ferris wheel with see-through floors. It is the fifth tallest ferris wheel in the world and the tallest in Japan.
277. In downtown Dallas, there is a thirty foot (nine meter) tall sculpture of an eyeball. It was created by multimedia artist Tony Tasset, from Chicago, in 2007, and it's located on the grounds of the Joule Hotel.
278. On August 20, 1977, Voyager II was launched; while on September 5, Voyager I was launched. They were sent on different trajectories and Voyager I was put on a path to reach Jupiter and Saturn ahead of Voyager II.
279. The abnormal fear of beautiful women is called caligynephobia, or venustraphobia, or for short Gynophobia.
280. Natal teeth is a term used to refer to babies who are born with teeth. According to the National Institution of Health, one out of every 2,000 to 3,000 babies is born with teeth.
281. George Lucas, the creator of Star Wars, made a pledge that stated he'd donate most of his money to improving education. Two years later in 2012, he sold his company Lucasfilm to Disney, and donated most of the money to a foundation that focuses on education.
282. Jean-Claude Van Damme was the original actor behind the scenes shot for the movie Predator. Because he didn't like the suit that he had to wear, he was then replaced by actor Kevin Peter Hall.
283. Napoleon wanted a form of communication in the early 19th century that would not require sound or light. It was created and named "tactile military code" which became the basis for braille.
284. In Japan, the macaque monkeys that inhabit Yakushima Island have been known to ride sika deer around like horses.
285. In an attempt to help reestablish some habitats, scientists are using 3D printing technology to create fake reefs. These are less vulnerable to climate change and more durable in changing ocean chemistry.
286. In the first National Collegiate Athletic Association (NCAA)

tournament, only eight teams participated. Since 2011, the number of teams has increased to sixty eight.

287. If a big disaster or a hacking group cause the Internet to crash, there are seven people in the world who have key cards that can reboot the system when five of the keys are used together. These people literally hold the keys to the worldwide Internet security.

288. Henry Cavill was playing World of Warcraft when he got a call from Zack Snyder for the role of Superman. He almost missed the call because of the game.

289. Acqua di Cristallo Tributo a Modigliani is the most expensive bottle of water in the world priced at sixty thousand dollars for twenty five ounces. It comes from either Fiji or France and is contained within a twenty four karat solid gold bottle.

290. In the United States, it's estimated that nearly 14.5 million people have survived cancer.

291. The closest state in the United States to Africa is Maine.

292. The largest country in the world that has no rivers is Saudi Arabia.

293. In the 13th century, Frederick II, emperor of Germany, wanted to find out which language humans would speak naturally, so he gave the care of fifty newborns to nurses who would only feed and bathe the babies, but were not allowed to speak or hold them. The emperor got no answer because all children eventually died.

294. A dead person can also get Goosebumps; however, they aren't triggered the same way as a living person. It can occur when "rigor mortis" sets in, which is when muscles contract and causes the body to stiffen up. There are tiny muscles beneath our hair follicles which also contract, causing the hair to stand on end and make it look to have Goosebumps.

295. Declaring and paying state tax on goods that have been bought online from out of state is supposedly a voluntary duty for all Americans. However, accountants and tax lawyers are some of the only people who actually pay it.

296. Pablo Escobar was a drug lord in Colombia who offered to pay

the countries $20 billion foreign debt to avoid being extradited to the US.
297. The largest female afro according to the Guinness World Records measures 7.2 inches (18.5 centimeters) high, 7.7 inches (19.6 centimeters) wide, and 52 inches (132 centimeters) in circumference. The record was achieved on October 4, 2010, by Eva Douglas in New Orleans, US.
298. In 1849, Elizabeth Blackwell was the first woman in the United States to receive a medical degree.
299. In the Back to the Future trilogy, Donald Trump was actually the inspiration for the character Biff Tanned.
300. On the Titanic, there were twelve confirmed dogs onboard, but only three of them survived.
301. To celebrate the 2016 Cheltenham Festival, designer Alexander McQueen's former apprentice, Emma Sandham-King, made the world's first Harris Tweed suit, specially designed for a horse. Four weeks and more than eighteen meters of tweed were needed to complete the three-piece suit, which was worn by a racehorse named Morestead.
302. The first major US city to require that all new buildings have solar panels installed on the roof was San Francisco.
303. In order to save money on expensive gasoline, Ukrainian drivers are converting their cars into being fueled by wood with burners instead of fuel tanks.
304. The swiftlet's nest is made out of the bird's own saliva. In some Asian countries, the bird's nest is boiled into a soup and it's considered a delicacy. A single bowl of soup can cost $100.
305. A German psychology study in the 1980's found that husbands who kiss their partner before leaving for work lived longer, earned more and had less car accidents.
306. "Alexander's band" or "Alexander's dark band" is the name of the dark band that you can see between the primary and secondary bows of a rainbow. It was named after Alexander of Aphrodisias who first described it in 200 AD.
307. Top soccer player Cristiano Ronaldo was asked to donate his cleats for a charity auction. The auction aimed to raise money for ten month old Erik Ortiz Cruz, who had a brain disorder

that could cause thirty seizures a day. Cristiano didn't donate the cleats, but he instead paid for the child's surgery, some $83,000.

308. An indoor farm was created in Japan that has the ability to create ten thousand heads of lettuce in a day, using 99% less water than an outdoor farm.

309. During the mummification process, ancient Egyptians sometimes used lichen and onions to fill the body's cavities and often reused that as fake eyes.

310. There is a device that allows monkeys to control robotic wheelchairs by sending signals with their brains. It was developed by scientists at Duke University with the aim of helping the elderly and people with disabilities.

311. The reason we can't see our own eyes in the mirror is because of something called saccadic masking. Our brain purposely blocks our vision in instances, otherwise our view would be like watching a video that's being shot with a shaky hand.

312. Artist Michael Pangrazio created the matte painting used to film the warehouse scene in "Raiders of the Lost Ark." It was painted on glass and the live action shots were actually done through a hole in it. It took him three months to complete it.

313. The IOS game "Clash of Clans" was making a remarkable one and a half million dollars a day at its peak.

314. Bob Marley suffered from racism when growing up as he was seen as a white man due to having a British father.

315. A type of transparent wood has been developed by scientists in Sweden. The wood can actually be used as windows.

316. Kiran Cable, a twenty year old man from South Wales, spent so much time with his girlfriend that his friends said that he actually disappeared from their lives. After eighteen months of unreturned calls and emails, Cable's friends decided to surprise him with a mock funeral that included a coffin, a hearse, and even an eulogy.

317. In Japan, a tiny drone has been used by researchers to pollinate a real flower. They achieved this by attaching horsehair bristles from a paintbrush to the bottom of the drone to imitate the fuzzy torso of a bee. Then they covered the hairs

with a sticky gel, which captures the pollen when it touches the flower.
318. The University of Warsaw found that the average human can track up to four moving things at one time, however, a gamer is able to track up to seven.
319. In December of 2016, and for the first time since 1979, it snowed in the Sahara Desert. The snow fell in the Atlas Mountains, in the northern edge of the Sahara Desert, and stayed for about a day.
320. The female with the longest legs in the world according to the Guinness World Records is Russian Svetlana Pankratova. As of July 8, 2003, her legs measured 4.3 feet (1.3 meters) long.
321. More than seventy separate pieces of wood are contained in a violin.
322. The man who invented the ATM, John Shepherd-Barron, wanted the machine to have a pin number of six digits originally. Since his wife could only remember four numbers at a time, that became the norm.
323. Witzelsucht, a German term that means joke addiction, is a type of condition that some people with brain disorders may suffer. Those afflicted have a compulsion to constantly tell jokes.
324. The toasted selfie is a device introduced by the Vermont Novelty Toaster Corporation. If you send them a selfie, they will print it for you on a selfie toast-producing gadget.
325. An Indonesian man named Mbah Gotho claims to be 146 years old. He actually has a photo of his government ID card that shows his birth date as December 31, 1870. He has outlived all ten of his siblings, four wives and his children.
326. Sensor Wake is an alarm clock that uses aromas of your choice to wake you up instead of sounds. You can be delightfully awoken by scents like cut grass, hot croissant, chocolate, espresso, or peppermint.
327. Sean's Bar is a pub located in Athlone, Ireland, that has been open since 900 AD.
328. The blackest black material which is able to absorb 99.96% of

visual light is called Vantablack. People who have seen this say it's like looking into an abyss.

329. On July 16, 1935, the "Park-O-Meter" was the world's first parking meter to be installed. It was set up on the southeast corner of what was then First Street and Robinson Avenue, in Oklahoma City.

330. Jackie Kennedy, former First American Lady, actually won an Emmy for her televised tour of the White House in 1962.

331. In 2014, Jason Willis, a thirty one year old American from Waterford, Wisconsin, was banned from the Internet after sending a naked man to a neighbor's house using a Craigslist ad.

332. Based on a report published in the Wall Street Journal in 2010, during a one hour regulation football game, the total of all plays averaged just eleven minutes.

333. Approximately one million people live in nuclear underground bunkers in Beijing, which have been transformed into housing units. They were originally built in the late 1960's and 1970's, in anticipation of the devastation of the Cold War nuclear fallout.

334. Skunks are actually immune to snake venom.

335. Cheetos Company joined the beauty market in 2016 when they produced a perfume called "Cheeteau" that smelled like Cheetos and retailed for nineteen dollars. They also produced a Cheetos themed bronzer that supposedly gave users the "Cheetos-kissed glow."

336. In 2014, a study done by scientists at the University of Wyoming in Laramie revealed that bumble bees can fly higher than Mount Everest. The bees were placed in a Plexiglas flight chamber and the air was pulled out of the chamber by using a hand pump to create the reduced air pressures that the bees would face at high altitudes. The Plexiglas broke before the bumble bees stopped flying.

337. Based on the different types of street lamps used to give off different shades of light, it is actually possible to differentiate between East and West Berlin from space.

338. Zambia is a country with very fertile lands, however, not much

agriculture grows there. This is because when there is any greenery, the hippos come out and eat everything.
339. In 1893, the Chicago World's Fair by George W. Ferris invented the first Ferris Wheel. It was 260 feet (seventy nine meters) high, cost fifty cents per ride, and could carry sixty passengers in each of the thirty six cars. That's a total capacity of 2,160 passengers.
340. The Titanic used to have its own newspaper called "The Atlantic Daily Bulletin." It was printed daily on board and it had news, ads, stock prices, horse racing results, gossip, and the day's menu.
341. The whale species with the thickest blubber of all is found on the bowhead whale, which lives exclusively in the Arctic. It can get as thick as twenty eight inches (seventy one centimeters).
342. In 2014, a parking space in London sold for 400,000 pounds. That's two and a half times the cost of the average UK home.
343. Edith Macefield was an eighty four year old lady who refused an offer of a million dollars from a building developer to move, so they built around her house instead. The movie "Up" was inspired by this story.
344. In 2006, a woman with a medical condition on a flight from Washington to Dallas was lighting matches to cover her own body odor. As the air staff couldn't detect where the smell was coming from, they were forced to land the plane in Nashville.
345. The Rosetta wearable disk is an archive of over 1,000 languages compressed using nanotechnology onto a less than one inch (2.54 centimeter) device pendant, created by the Rosetta Project. You can only read it with the use of a microscope and you can only get one if you donate $1,000 to the foundation.
346. There is a type of fish known as the "barreleye" that has a completely transparent head. It inhabits depths of around 2,000 feet (600 meters) to 2,600 feet (800 meters) where it's almost absolute black.
347. Italian wine company Torti Winery has teamed up with Sanrio, the company that created the Hello Kitty character, to create a line of Hello Kitty wine. It is a blend of Pinot Noir

and Chardonnay. According to Torti, every grape is handpicked.

348. In the past, the twenty fourth floor of the Empire State Building was furnished with special comfortable chairs called "nap pods," in which people could take twenty minute siestas.

349. Elephants can hold and store on average of a gallon (four liters) of water in their trunks.

350. Muhammad Ali once invited Billy Crystal to join him for a run at the local country club. Billy accepted, however, couldn't go because the country club didn't allow Jews. Ali never went back to that club.

351. In order to help calm anxious mothers, the Hao Sheng Hospital in Japan decorated their maternity ward in 2006 with Hello Kitty-themed murals and items. The cartoon image is on everything, from walls to newborn baby blankets. In the entrance lobby, there's even a giant Hello Kitty figure dressed in a pink doctor's uniform that greets visitors.

352. Having more stainless steel in your kitchen reduces the amount of odor from garlic or onion.

353. The first parliament in the world to be completely powered by solar energy is Pakistan's Parliament.

354. In 2002, a Hooters in Panama City, Florida, offered employees a chance to win a Toyota. Jodee Berry, the winning waitress, was given a toy Yoda action figure as a prank, so she sued the company and won enough to buy any type of Toyota she wanted.

355. Rick Astley became an Internet sensation in 2007 with his video "Never Gonna Give You Up", when it became part of an Internet prank known as "Rickrolling." Unfortunately, he didn't claim ownership of his work and earned only $12 in royalties off of his nearly 150 million YouTube views.

356. In the past, in order to cure head lice, gasoline, kerosene, benzene, and turpentine were all used as treating substances. References to it appear in medical journals as far back as 1917.

357. Cobwebs actually have antifungal and antiseptic properties that keep bacteria away and minimize the chance of infection. In fact, the Greeks and Romans would use cobwebs to treat cuts

in ancient times. Soldiers also used them to heal wounds, combining honey and vinegar to clean the lesions, and then covering them with balled-up spider webs.

358. In South Korea, winning gold at the Asian Games or any medal at the Olympics will exempt any able-bodied males from the country's mandatory military service.

359. The most expensive potato chip in the world is crafted by a Swedish brewery. It costs $56 for a set of five or $11.20 per piece. They are made from special potatoes that are hand-harvested, and come in five flavors: matsutake mushrooms, truffle seaweed, crown dill, Leksand onions, and Indian Pale Ale.

360. As of 2019, the total amount for US student loans hit a trillion dollars. This is bigger than some countries' whole economies.

361. "Pennywise Poo Poo Butt Inc" is the corporate name for Blink-182 which they chose so their accountants and managers would have to say that while doing business.

362. As they grow, bullfrogs periodically shed their skin at regular intervals. In fact, the old skin is pushed off with their hind legs and eaten by them.

363. George Barbe, a billionaire from Alabama, had several life sized dinosaurs built and placed over his ten thousand acre home in 1991.

364. Superior canal dissonance is a condition where sufferers can hear their own pulse and their eyes moving in their sockets.

365. Andrew Johnson and Bill Clinton are the only two US presidents who have been impeached so far. However, neither of them was convicted of charges filed against them.

366. The tropical cycads known as Lepidozamia and Encephalartos create the world's largest African pine cones, measuring almost 3.28 feet (one meter) in length and weighing up to ninety nine pounds (forty five kilograms).

367. The kangaroo rats that live in deserts can go their whole lives without drinking any water. They get enough moisture from their seed diet to survive.

368. In 2015, selfie sticks were banned in Disney parks for safety

reasons, as the long arms could collide with a ride's mechanism or stick another guest.

369. The puffer fish, known also as blowfish, has enough toxins in it to kill thirty adult humans, and there is no antidote. Incredibly, the meat of some puffer fish is considered a delicacy in some parts of the world.

370. Since 1996, Harold Hackett has thrown 4,871 messages in a bottle from Prince Edward Island, Canada. He has actually received 3,100 responses, which represents a 63.6% response rate.

371. In 2014, the largest pyramid constructed with coins was built in Lithuania, made from over a million coins.

372. The color purple was known as a royal color in history due to the fact that they relied on dyes back then and it was so hard to obtain that only the royals could afford it. It was only found from the sea and took twelve thousand snails to produce only one and a half grams of purple dye.

373. There's a roller coaster in Japan known as the "Sky Cycle" where you actually have to pedal yourself to propel yourself forward through the track.

374. The largest weight loss documented for a human was by John Minnoch who weighed 1,400 pounds (635kg) and lost 924 pounds (419kg).

375. After being decapitated for hours, poisonous snakes could still bite, inject venom, and kill you. According to Steven Beaupre, biology professor at the University of Arkansas, snakes can retain reflexes after death and for venomous snakes, like cobras and rattlesnakes, biting is one of those reflexes.

376. Approximately 80% of Americans have siblings. Older siblings tend to be less extroverted than younger siblings. Although the siblings tend to resemble each other in looks and intelligence, they have quite different personalities.

377. If you drop a steel ball and a rubber ball, both of the same size, from the same height, the steel ball will actually bounce higher as it snaps back to its original shape faster than the rubber ball.

378. On a few occasions, a hen will lay an egg inside of an egg. It occurs when a hen is in the process of forming an egg in her

oviduct and a second oocyte is released by the ovary before the first egg has completely traveled through the oviduct and been laid.

379. After calculating population density, unemployment rates, hours worked, and other factors, a study conducted by the real estate website Movoto found that Florida is currently America's most stressed-out state.

380. In the rainforests of New Guinea, two new types of ants were discovered by scientists, which were named Pheidole Viserion and Pheidole Drogon, after the fire breathing dragons from the fantasy series Game of Thrones. The ants bear a strong resemblance to the dragons because they have blade-like serrations on their backs.

381. The world record for the largest ball of chewing gum is held by Barry Chapelle from Los Angeles. Over a six year period, he chewed 95,200 pieces of Nicorette gum, forming it into a giant gumball that weighs more than 174 pounds (seventy nine kilograms) and measures over 4.9 feet (1.5 meters) in circumference.

382. Proxima Centauri is the closest star to Earth, which is 4.24 light-years away. A single light-year is 5.86 million miles (9.44 trillion kilometers).

383. There is a museum in Yokohama City, Japan, dedicated entirely to ramen noodles. It's called the Shin-Yokohama Raumen Museum.

384. There are more than 3,200 confirmed new planets that have been discovered by telescope.

385. The national animal of North Korea is the Chollima, a mythical winged horse.

386. The only country that doesn't feature its name on its stamps is the United Kingdom. However, all UK stamps do have a picture of the monarch's head.

387. All residents of Alaska receive an oil royalty check each year for their share of revenue from Alaskan oil. The payment is usually between one and two thousand dollars.

388. Pikachurin Protein was named by Japanese scientists after the Pokemon character Pikachu because of the character's agility.

389. Due to evolution, human brains have gotten bigger and our intelligence has increased while our muscles have become smaller and weaker.
390. In 2016, a study done by the laundry detergent brand Persil in the UK revealed that kids in the United Kingdom spend less time outside than prisoners. The survey of 2,000 British parents found that nearly three-quarters of children are spending less than one hour outside every day, and 20% don't go outside on a regular basis at all. However, British inmates receive at least one hour of suitable exercise outdoors every day.
391. In 2006, a study done by Alex Thornton and Katherine McAuliffe at Cambridge University showed how adult meerkats teach their youngest pups how not to be stung by scorpions, one of their main sources of prey. First, they bring dead scorpions to the pups; then they bring ones that are alive but injured; and, eventually, they work there way up to live prey.
392. The creator of Wendy's, Dave Thomas, worked at KFC before he started, and was the one who designed the signature KFC bucket.
393. In the 1940's, the first beer ever to be sold in a six-pack was Pabst Blue Ribbon Beer.
394. Approximately one in 200 people are born with an extra rib called a cervical rib. At the back, it connects to the seven cervical vertebrae in your neck. At the front, in some people, the rib can be floating and have no connection. Similarly, it can be connected to your first rib by a band of tough fibrous tissue, or there may be a joint to connect it to your first rib. It can also be just on the right side, just on the left side, or even both sides.
395. Apollo 16 astronaut Charles Duke was the youngest man in history to walk on the moon at the age of thirty six. He left a photo of his family on the moon with the inscription: "This is the family of astronaut Charlie Duke, from the planet Earth, who landed on the moon on April 20, 1972." The picture still remains on the moon surface.

396. In 2008, the first known coffee plant that contains no caffeine was discovered. It was named coffea charrieriana.
397. In 1974, Gerber baby products tried to market meals in a jar, like creamed beef and beef burgundy, aimed to college students and young adults. Unfortunately, the product failed.
398. In 2014, a mobile game was released called "Run Forrest Run," based on the movie Forrest Gump, where you run through Forrest's entire life.
399. Before the game, all NHL hockey pucks are frozen so that they glide smoother and faster during the game.
400. In Norway, there is a sauna that can house 150 people. It's a large timber construction set on a beach, which overlooks the Arctic Ocean.
401. Some cats and dogs can actually be allergic to human dander. Dander is made up of tiny cells shed from hair, fur, or feathers. Although it's known to be related with pets, humans can produce it too.
402. In January of 1966, Spain was accidentally bombed by the US. Four nuclear weapons were carried by an Air Force bomber when it collided with its refueling tanker over the Spanish town of Palomares, sending the bombs screaming towards the ground.
403. A hamdog is a hamburger and hotdog combination with a special shaped bun, created by Australian Mark Murray.
404. In 1934, Hawaiian Punch was originally developed as an ice cream topping. Later on, it became the tropical fruit drink when consumers discovered how good it was when mixed with water.
405. In South Korea, there is a plastic surgery called smile lipping, where both corners of your mouth are raised in order to give you a permanent smile.
406. The last words of famous writer H.G. Wells were "Go away, I'm alright."
407. Disney Parks can actually deny people access to their parks if they find that they have a questionable tattoo.
408. In the Satere-Mawe Indian culture, there is an initiation ritual for thirteen year old boys that consists of making them wear

389. Due to evolution, human brains have gotten bigger and our intelligence has increased while our muscles have become smaller and weaker.
390. In 2016, a study done by the laundry detergent brand Persil in the UK revealed that kids in the United Kingdom spend less time outside than prisoners. The survey of 2,000 British parents found that nearly three-quarters of children are spending less than one hour outside every day, and 20% don't go outside on a regular basis at all. However, British inmates receive at least one hour of suitable exercise outdoors every day.
391. In 2006, a study done by Alex Thornton and Katherine McAuliffe at Cambridge University showed how adult meerkats teach their youngest pups how not to be stung by scorpions, one of their main sources of prey. First, they bring dead scorpions to the pups; then they bring ones that are alive but injured; and, eventually, they work there way up to live prey.
392. The creator of Wendy's, Dave Thomas, worked at KFC before he started, and was the one who designed the signature KFC bucket.
393. In the 1940's, the first beer ever to be sold in a six-pack was Pabst Blue Ribbon Beer.
394. Approximately one in 200 people are born with an extra rib called a cervical rib. At the back, it connects to the seven cervical vertebrae in your neck. At the front, in some people, the rib can be floating and have no connection. Similarly, it can be connected to your first rib by a band of tough fibrous tissue, or there may be a joint to connect it to your first rib. It can also be just on the right side, just on the left side, or even both sides.
395. Apollo 16 astronaut Charles Duke was the youngest man in history to walk on the moon at the age of thirty six. He left a photo of his family on the moon with the inscription: "This is the family of astronaut Charlie Duke, from the planet Earth, who landed on the moon on April 20, 1972." The picture still remains on the moon surface.

396. In 2008, the first known coffee plant that contains no caffeine was discovered. It was named coffea charrieriana.
397. In 1974, Gerber baby products tried to market meals in a jar, like creamed beef and beef burgundy, aimed to college students and young adults. Unfortunately, the product failed.
398. In 2014, a mobile game was released called "Run Forrest Run," based on the movie Forrest Gump, where you run through Forrest's entire life.
399. Before the game, all NHL hockey pucks are frozen so that they glide smoother and faster during the game.
400. In Norway, there is a sauna that can house 150 people. It's a large timber construction set on a beach, which overlooks the Arctic Ocean.
401. Some cats and dogs can actually be allergic to human dander. Dander is made up of tiny cells shed from hair, fur, or feathers. Although it's known to be related with pets, humans can produce it too.
402. In January of 1966, Spain was accidentally bombed by the US. Four nuclear weapons were carried by an Air Force bomber when it collided with its refueling tanker over the Spanish town of Palomares, sending the bombs screaming towards the ground.
403. A hamdog is a hamburger and hotdog combination with a special shaped bun, created by Australian Mark Murray.
404. In 1934, Hawaiian Punch was originally developed as an ice cream topping. Later on, it became the tropical fruit drink when consumers discovered how good it was when mixed with water.
405. In South Korea, there is a plastic surgery called smile lipping, where both corners of your mouth are raised in order to give you a permanent smile.
406. The last words of famous writer H.G. Wells were "Go away, I'm alright."
407. Disney Parks can actually deny people access to their parks if they find that they have a questionable tattoo.
408. In the Satere-Mawe Indian culture, there is an initiation ritual for thirteen year old boys that consists of making them wear

gloves made of bullet ants for ten minutes. Although they are repeatedly bitten, which is incredibly painful, they must not cry out if they want to be declared a man.

409. The leading cause for accidental deaths in 2014 wasn't the usual car crashes but accidental drug overdoses.

410. Iron Nun is the nickname given to eighty six year old nun Madonna Buder due to her amazing endurance. She has completed more than forty Iron Man races, which consist of a 111.7 mile (180 kilometer) bike ride, 2.4 mile (3.9 kilometer) swim, and a 26.2-mile (42.2 kilometer) run. She is, in fact, the oldest Iron Man triathlon competitor.

411. Photographer Hallgrimur Pierre Helgason once captured stunning images of the Aurora Borealis over Iceland just at the moment they formed the outline of a phoenix.

412. Due to a huge earthquake in Nepal in 2015, Mount Everest shrank by an inch.

413. A kindle is the name given to a group of kittens with the same mother.

414. In the original "The Wizard of Oz book", Dorothy's magical slippers were actually silver and not ruby red as in the movie. The color was changed because it was believed that they would be more notable against the yellow brick road.

415. The oldest acting parliament in the world is the parliament of Iceland, which was founded back in 930 AD. Political gatherings typically lasted for two weeks, during the month of June, which was a period of continuous daylight and nice weather.

416. Pigs are actually very intelligent animals and have the ability to even manipulate purposefully. For example, they can pinpoint a weak spot, remember it, and use it to their advantage later on.

417. In the movie Jurassic Park, the sound of Velociraptors talking back and forth to each other was actually the sound of mating tortoises.

418. When Jason Padgett was a kid, he had a hard time studying algebra or math. After being attacked outside of a bar however, he started seeing the world in pixelated, geometric shapes. He soon realized about his new ability, understood right away the

concept of Pi, and hand drew complex fractals, becoming a renowned math genius.
419. Most cats don't like water with the exception of the fishing cat, which is found in India. The main part of the fishing cat's diet is made of fish, so they are experts in swimming and diving, as well as scooping them out with their paws.
420. Approximately 2.3 million people around the world are employed by Walmart.
421. In Peru, it's a New Year's tradition to give and wear new yellow underwear. It actually represents luck and happiness.
422. Ground bees in China can be used as a natural remedy for a sore throat.
423. The Harry Potter series has been translated into more than seventy languages.
424. If you were to be born on a plane flying above the US, you would automatically be given citizenship, however, if you were born over an ocean, it would depend on which country the plane is registered.
425. In the village of Al Walaja, within the Bethlehem district of Palestine, there is an olive tree that is over 4,000 years old. It was named Al Badawi, after a wise villager who lived in Al Walaja over 200 years ago. The tree is thirty nine feet (eleven meters) tall and eighty two feet (twenty five meters) in diameter, and is compared to that of ten average sized olive trees put together.
426. There is a wine fountain in the town of Caldari di Ortona, in Italy, that stays open twenty four hours a day.
427. The only two English words that both begin and end in "und" are underground and underfund.
428. Tunarama is an annual festival celebrated in Port Lincoln, Australia. The main event is the world championship tuna toss competition. The one who can throw their tuna the farthest is the winner.
429. In the last sixty years, Mexico City has sunk more than 32.1 feet (9.8 meters). This is because 70% of the water people rely on is extracted from the aquifer located below the city.
430. The first African American child to attend an all-white public

elementary school in the American South was six year old Ruby Nell Bridges, in November of 1960. For her safety, she had to be escorted to school by federal marshals and spent the first year as the only student in her class.

431. Based on a study done by Aric Prather, assistant professor of psychiatry at the University of California, people are four times more likely to get a cold if they get less than six hours of sleep per night.

432. The fear of cooking is called mageirocophobia. It's a very common affection that can take many forms, although it is only considered a phobia when it's severe enough to interfere with daily life.

433. The Church of Scientology has been in the country of Germany since the 1970's, however, the German government doesn't recognize it as a religion and only as an abusive business that's masquerading as religion.

434. In the past, many movie theaters used to have cry rooms where you could place your children if they were giving you trouble. This way you could still enjoy the movie while not disturbing others.

435. Over the reign of Queen Elizabeth II, she has owned more than thirty Corgis.

436. A sixteen year old Russian powerlifter, Maryana Naumova, can bench press 350 pounds (160kg).

437. The real name of Ulysses S. Grant, the 18th president of the United States, was actually Hiram Ulysses Grant. The middle initial "S" meant nothing and it was the result of an error from Ohio Congressman Thomas Hammer; he accidentally wrote his name as Ulysses S. Grant when he was nominated to attend West Point.

438. Christian Poincheval created a variety of pills that made people's fart smell like roses or chocolates, in 2014. He named the chocolate one "Father Christmas Fart Pill."

439. The very first message sent between two computers over the Internet was back in 1969, and it was "lo." The complete message was supposed to be "login", but the computer crashed after the first two letters.

440. A stray cat became the seeing eye guide for a dog named Terfel who went blind in 2012; the cat uses its paws to guide the dog around the house
441. Based on research done by the Royal Society for Public Health, approximately 800 additional calories a week are consumed by the average UK commuter while traveling to and from work, as a consequence from consuming mostly unhealthy snacks.
442. Elimination communication is a technique where, instead of using diapers, parents learn to use timing, signals, and cues to know when their baby needs to pee or poo.
443. The patron saint of Ireland, Saint Patrick, wasn't actually Irish. Although the exact birth place and date is unknown, it is believed that he was born around 375 A.D. in Scotland, and his real name is believed to be Maewyn Succat, taking the name Patrick upon becoming a priest.
444. In Japan, nearly 1,500 earthquakes are recorded every year.
445. A senator named Larry Pressler refused a bribe offered to him from the FBI in the 1970's. He was called a hero for his act, but he didn't think that refusing the bribe should be considered a heroic act.
446. Gimpie Gimpie is a bush that's known to sting anyone who touches it by delivering a potent neurotoxin. The fruit however is edible if the stingers are removed.
447. In Illinois there is a company called the "Second Chance Coffee Company" that only hires ex-inmates as employees. The company actually conducts FBI background checks to make sure that those seeking employment in the company have actually been to prison.
448. The most famous opera singer of the late Victorian period was Dame Nellie Melba. Melba toast and peach melba are actually both named after her.
449. The tumbler for the Dark Knight trilogy is not a CGI model; it's actually a working vehicle.
450. According to a 2014 report from the United States Department of Agriculture, the average American consumes up to 170 pounds (seventy seven kilograms) of refined sugar every year.
451. Dr. Seuss' first book was rejected twenty seven times. He was

almost ready to give up but one day he bumped into a friend on the street in New York City, back in 1937, who had just begun working in publishing. Seuss said that if he had been walking on the other side of the street, he probably would have never been a children's author.

452. The first female flight attendant ever was Ellen Church, who began flying in 1930. She implemented a plan that required all flight attendants to be registered nurses. However, when World War II began, all nurses were enlisted in the war, so most airlines simply dropped the requirement in order to find any workers.

453. Instead of front teeth, cows, sheep, and goats all have a tough dental pad below their top lip. This dental arrangement helps them gather great quantities of grass and fibrous plants.

454. "Mutton shunters" was the name given to police in Victorian times.

455. In the early 1900's, "Tug of War" used to be an Olympic sport.

456. A third grade girl was expelled from school for a year for carrying a dangerous weapon. Her grandmother made a birthday cake for her and sent her to school along with the cake and a knife to cut it. The teacher used the knife to cut the cake and then reported the girl to the school authorities.

457. Back in 1995, Dwayne "The Rock" Johnson used to play football for the CFL's Calgary Stampeders. That was before he went into wrestling and acting.

458. The petals of skeleton flowers are so delicate that they become transparent when it rains.

459. In Hong Kong, there is a KFC that offers lickable edible fingernail polish in two different flavors: "original" and "hot and spicy."

460. The largest desert on Earth is the Antarctic Polar Desert, which covers the continent of Antarctica and is the size of about 5.5 million square miles (8.8 square kilometers).

461. The cartoon on the Cap'n Crunch cereal is not really a captain, but a commander. Real captains have four stripes on their sleeves, but the cartoon only has three which makes him a commander.

462. Given the continual complaints from customers about their phones catching on fire, Samsung had to stop the production and sales of its Galaxy Note Seven Smartphone. Even when they attempted to replace the battery supplier, customers still reported the same issues. They were forced to recall 2.5 million phones.
463. In the early 20th century, it was possible to order a kit from the Sears catalog to build a house. Some of the types of constructions offered were small bungalows, large farmhouses, and Queen Anne style homes. All the parts and materials were included in the kit, which were all delivered by train.
464. The average umbilical cord measures about twenty inches (fifty centimeters).
465. Aquagenic urticarial is a rare condition that causes sufferers to break out in hives when their skin comes in contact with water no matter its temperature. Doctors are still in doubt as to what causes it.
466. Declawing your cat is illegal in most European countries, including Britain. In Israel, for example, if you're caught declawing a cat, you can be sent to prison for a year and be fined twenty thousand dollars. Over thirty other countries, including Scotland, Italy, and New Zealand, have also followed suit.
467. On February 13, 2017, a study released by Netflix revealed that almost half of streaming couples around the world have cheated on their significant other by watching a show ahead of them without their knowledge.
468. The Hubble Space Telescope travels around the Earth taking pictures of the stars, planets, and galaxies at about 24,928 feet (7,600 meters) per second.
469. Dogs don't feel some emotions such as shame and guilt, however do feel sadness when they get shouted at from owners.
470. The "Old Man of the Lake" is a floating tree trunk located in Crater Lake, in Central Oregon. The tree has been bobbing completely vertically in the lake for over a hundred years. It has even been referenced in writing as far back as 1896.

471. Brazilian soccer great Pele was actually convinced by US politician Henry Kissinger to play in the United States.
472. Robert Emmet Odlum, a professional high-diver, was the first person to jump off of the Brooklyn Bridge. He wanted to prove that people did not die by simply falling through the air, so he jumped off the bridge falling 130 feet (41 meters) safely through the air. Unfortunately, he died when he hit the water.
473. If you immerse a pearl in vinegar, it will actually dissolve as it is mostly calcium carbonate, which is susceptible to even the weakest acid solution.
474. In Tonopa, Nevada, there is a clown motel decorated with hundreds of clowns. It's located right next to a graveyard.
475. The only one of the seven wonders of the ancient world that still exists is the Great Pyramid of Giza, in Egypt. The rest were all destroyed, including the Colossus of Rhodes, the Lighthouse of Alexandria, the Mausoleum at Halicarnassus, the Temple of Artemis, and the Statue of Zeus.
476. Aphantasia is a condition where sufferers are unable to create visualisations in their minds.
477. The reason why Napoleon Bonaparte wore his black, felted, beaver fur hat sideways, instead of with the points at the front and back, was so that he could be easily spotted on the battlefield.
478. The "Highway HiFi" was a record player offered by Chrysler in its new cars from 1956 to 1958. However, because they had a tendency to break, the device was later removed.
479. In ancient Egypt, if a cat would pass away, the members of the family would shave their eyebrows off in mourning.
480. In Japan, there is a service consisting of hiring a handsome man who will show up at your office, sit down next to you, watch sad videos with you until you cry, and then he will wipe away your tears for you.
481. The Sobrino de Botin is the world's oldest restaurant, located in Madrid, Spain, and was founded in 1725 by French cook Jean Botin and his wife.
482. In August 2016, a limited edition Swedish Fish Oreo cookie

was released by Nabisco. It's the regular chocolate cookie but filled with a red Swedish Fish flavored cream.

483. There was a belief that Communist firing squads were not permitted to shoot at an image of their leaders. For that reason, Russian criminals used to get tattoos bearing the images of Lenin and Stalin so they wouldn't get shot.

484. One of the two non-human primates that have blue eyes is the blue-eyed black lemur. They are among one of the twenty five most endangered primates. In fact, conservationists think that there are only between 450 to 2,500 in the whole world.

485. To attract females the male kangaroos flex their biceps and wrestle other males to show their dominance.

486. Originally, the word outlaw meant "outside the protection of the law." In other words, you could rob or kill without having legal consequences.

487. Starfish, or sea stars, have no brain and no blood. Their nervous system is actually spread through their arms and their blood is filtered sea water.

488. Coincidentally, astronaut Buzz Aldrin's middle name was Moon.

489. Jerome Rodale was a longevity expert and the father of organic farming. During an interview at the age of seventy one, he announced that he had decided to live to be 100, declaring that he had never felt better in life. Minutes later he died of a heart attack while still filming.

490. Architects in Iceland wanted utility towers to go beyond their basic functional structures, so they created a design proposal called "The Land of Giants." Basically, it turns electrical pylons into human-shaped sculptures.

491. Conflict Kitchen is a restaurant located in Pittsburgh that only serves cuisine from countries that the US is in conflict with. When they started serving Palestinian food, they received death threats.

492. Chuck Lorre, the creator of "The Big Bang Theory," and "Two and a Half Men," also wrote "The Teenage Mutant Ninja Turtles" theme song.

493. The first nation to start switching off its FM radio network and taking the jump to digital technology was Norway.
494. "The Bikers Against Child Abuse," or "BACA," is a group of bikers who escort abused children to therapy sessions or school to help them feel safer and supported. They even sometimes attend the courtroom cases where victims testify against their abusers.
495. The Great Sphinx of Giza was constructed out of a single chunk of soft limestone bedrock. This magnificent monument stands over sixty five feet (twenty meters) high, almost 240 feet (seventy four meters) long, and over sixty two feet (nineteen meters) wide.
496. An underground chamber containing over 8,000 life-sized warrior figures made out of terracotta clay was found by local farmers when drilling for water in the Shaanxi province of China, in March of 1974. The chamber belonged to China's first emperor Qin Shi Huang, who ordered the construction of the figures back in 246 B.C., in readiness for his own burial; he was only thirteen years old at the time.
497. There are twenty three official languages in India. Although Hindi is the official language of the Indian central government, and English is a provisional official sub language, all other individual state legislatures are free to adopt any regional language as the official language of that state.
498. Alpacas have been known to die of loneliness. This is why you usually always see them in groups.
499. Before 1970, the exclamation mark was not part of the keyboard. Before it was added that year, you would have to type a full stop, then hit the "backspace" key to move back before adding an apostrophe over the full stop.
500. In 1928, Madeline Scotto graduated from an elementary school which she came back and taught at as a teacher continuing to work there until 2015, when she was 101 years old.
501. The WWE superstar John Cena has granted more than 400 Make-A-Wish requests, more than anyone else in the charity's history.

502. Sunflowers are actually a cluster of dozens of little flowers as each petal is a single-petaled flower.
503. There is a tradition among military commandos in Lebanon of eating live snakes in order to display their strength and courage.
504. Congenital amusia is a type of disorder where people can't recognize common songs from their culture, can't differentiate when notes are out of tune, and sometimes say that music sounds like banging to them.
505. Elvis Presley made his first and last Grand Ole Opry appearance on October 2, 1954. Seemingly, his gyration-filled performance was not received well and one of the officials there apparently told him to not quit his day job, which was driving trucks.
506. After the movie "Cannibal Holocaust" was released in 1980, the director had to prove in court that the actors were indeed still alive and didn't die during the movie.
507. "Som Biotech Research Foundation" is a dog cloning service in South Korea that will actually clone your beloved pooch for around $100,000.
508. On March 1, 1950, the Westside Baptist Church in Beatrice, Nebraska, was affected by an explosion at 7:25 p.m. that destroyed the church. That night, the choir practice had been scheduled to begin at 7:20, however, one of the fifteen people who should have been present was injured, and as a result, all of them arrived late that night. Some people thought of it as a divine intervention.
509. Based on a report provided by the Center for Disease Control and Prevention's National Center for Health Statistics, today American men weigh on average 196 pounds (eighty nine kilograms), which is fifteen pounds (6.8 kilograms) more than twenty years ago. Additionally, women weigh 168 pounds (seventy six kilograms) on average, which is sixteen pounds (7.2 kilograms) more than twenty years ago.
510. During the Nigerian Civil War in 1967, both sides agreed to a forty eight hour ceasefire to be able to watch a soccer game.

They wanted to watch famous player "Pele" play, without having to worry about the war.

511. In Zhengzhou, China, there is a Korean restaurant where people don't have to pay for their meal if they're the five most attractive customers of that day.
512. The "your mother insult" is found in nearly all cultures and is as old as humanity itself; it can even be found in Shakespeare texts and the Bible.
513. The largest prehistoric man-made mound in Europe is found in Silbury Hill, near Avebury in Wiltshire, England. It stands 130 feet (thirty nine meters) high and its purpose is still unknown.
514. The Soviets built an A-40 Krylya Tanka, a tank that had wings during the Second World War. Luckily it didn't work.
515. A study done in 2013 showed that fans of Harry Potter were more politically tolerant, open to diversity, less authoritarian and less likely to support the use of torture or deadly force.
516. John F. Kennedy's older sister, Rosemary Kennedy, was lobotomized at the age of twenty three; the surgery failed and left her permanently incapacitated. The incident, however, inspired her sister, Eunice Kennedy Shriver, to launch the Special Olympics.
517. You could hear a hyena's laugh if you were sitting eight miles (thirteen kilometers) away.
518. Cocoa beans were often used by the Aztec natives as currency.
519. In 1848, an ice jam in the upper part of the river from Niagara Falls caused the falls to stay bone-dry for almost forty eight hours. Some people thought of it as a sign that the world was ending and attended special services at local churches. Niagara Falls has the highest flow rate of any waterfall in the world and delivers 4.4 gigawatts of energy to the area.
520. Usain Bolt found Chinese food to be rather odd when he was there for the 2008 Olympics so he only ate chicken nuggets. He still went on and won three gold medals.
521. Before 1987, surgeries performed on infants were done without anaesthesia as they believed that kids weren't able to feel pain.
522. In Washington, the American capitol subway system is a transit

system exclusively used by members of the Congress and Capitol Hill staff members.
523. Oscar the Grouch from Sesame Street wasn't always green; he was originally orange.
524. In 1952, President Harry Truman started the tradition of top secret intelligence briefings, a tradition still practiced to this day. He wanted to make sure that his successor was better prepared than he was, so he offered classified briefings to each of the nominees.
525. The first technical fatality of the Civil War occurred during a 100-gun salute. It happened when a cannon prematurely discharged, killing Private Daniel Hough of the First US Artillery.
526. The Polypterus is a kind of fish raised by researchers at McGill University in Montreal, Canada. It can breathe air and walk on land using its front fins.
527. A discovery made by the University of Wisconsin has led to the replacement of toxic and non-biodegradable materials in smartphones such as microchips. They have found a replacement material that's made from wood pulp that is both transparent and flexible.
528. In 2009, a study led by Deborah Wells of Queen's University, Belfast, discovered that female cats are often right-pawed while males are left-pawed. In humans, testosterone is related to left-handedness, which seems to apply to cats too.
529. "Too Good to Go" is an app that connects users to local restaurants in the United Kingdom that want to sell perfectly good leftover food at a much cheaper price.
530. Paper cuts often bleed very little or not at all and leave the skin's pain receptors open to the air, which is the reason why they hurt so much.
531. Jia Haixia, a double amputee, and Jim Wenqi, a blind man, with combined efforts have planted over ten thousand trees in Northern China and plan on planting another ten thousand.
532. Diving bell spiders can breathe underwater by using air bubbles. The bubbles act like mini scuba diving tanks.
533. In 2015, the National Fire Protection Association reported

1,345,500 fires in the United States alone. In fact, the number grows by almost 4% every year.

534. Queen Elizabeth is considered the first head of state to have used electronic mail. She sent her first email on March 26, 1976; the message was transmitted over ARPANET, the forerunner for the modern Internet.

535. In 2014, during a racing competition, a stray dog named Arthur followed a Swedish racing team through the Amazonian jungle and rivers, completing a 427 mile (688 kilometer) race, just because one of the team members had given it a meatball during one of the earlier halts.

536. Smoked bats are considered a delicacy in Indonesia.

537. In Italy, there is a vending machine named "Let's Pizza" that can create a fresh pizza in three minutes with custom toppings.

538. Soviet dictator Joseph Stalin had an accident involving a horse-drawn carriage when he was only twelve years old, which caused his left arm to be distinctly shorter than his right arm. His arm had to be reconstructed by surgery, leaving it shorter and stiffened at the elbow.

539. The Margate Grotto is a series of underground passageways located in Margate, England, that are covered in millions of sea shells. It was discovered in 1835, but it's still unknown how old the grotto really is or who built it.

540. The skull that Russians kept as proof of Hitler's death actually belongs to a woman.

541. To hard-boil an ostrich egg, it can take from 90 - 120 minutes.

542. On Marajo Island, Brazilian police ride water buffalos when they patrol the streets instead of horses.

543. As part of the management training program, NASA often shows the Hollywood movie Armageddon and then asks its new staff to identify as many scientific inaccuracies as they can. There are at least 168 of them.

544. In France, it is against the law that grocery stores throw away edible food. Instead, they have to donate edible, unused food to charity or other facilities that process it into animal feed or compost.

545. The word Kia is derived from the Chinese language. The first

syllable "Ki" means to arise or come out of. The second part of the word refers to Asia. So, basically, Kia means to rise up or come out of Asia.

546. A study conducted by TDG Research revealed that the average Netflix subscriber spends more than 550 hours every year using the service.

547. In downtown Austin, Minnesota, there is a museum dedicated to Spam. It has bluegrass instruments made of Spam cans, a Spam rocket, a Spam can conveyor suspended from the ceiling, and a Spam children's play area.

548. J. Paul Getty, one of the richest men of all time from the oil and gas industry, had a pay phone installed in his house after visitors racked up his phone bill.

549. In Sweden, there are winter concerts where all instruments are made of ice. They are considered some of the rarest instruments in the world and are actually very fragile; just a player's breath risks nudging them out of tune.

550. The Malm Whale is the only known mounted whale in the world. It is on display in Sweden's Natural History Museum. It was found stranded on rocks on October 29, 1865, when it swam too close to land in Askim Bay south of Goteborg. It was over fifty two feet (15.8 meters) long and weighed around twenty five tons.

551. The game hopscotch has its origin in ancient Britain, during the Roman Empire. The original courts were ninety eight feet (thirty meters) long and were used for military exercising. Soldiers used to run in full armor and field packs to improve their footwork. Later on, Roman children drew their own, smaller courts and added a scoring system; and thus, hopscotch was born and spread throughout Europe.

552. The record for one of the largest casts ever is held by the movie Gandhi. Just in the funeral scene, more than 300,000 people were used as extras.

553. German scientist Dan Frost has literally made a diamond out of peanut butter. While trying to create crystalline structures like those in Earth's lower mantle, he actually discovered how to form diamonds out of substances high in carbon.

554. In 1856, after trick photography was developed, creating headless portraits became a trend that swept through the Victorian era.
555. Pickles are served with sandwiches in restaurants because the acid in the vinegar works as a palate cleanser.
556. William Mckinley won the US election in 1896 by campaigning only on his front porch while his opponent spoke at over 600 events.
557. The first time in Olympic history that a South American country hosted the games was at the 2016 Olympics in Rio, Brazil.
558. Some companies in England are now offering pawternity, payed time off to take care of a pet in need.
559. At an anti-helmet rally event, motorcyclist Philip A. Contos died after he flipped over his handlebars and hit his head on the pavement.
560. Technically, the eyewear industry is monopolized by one Italian company: Luxottica Spa, which owns brands such as Ray-Ban, Persol, and Oakley. They also make glasses for Chanel, Prada, Armani, Burberry, Versace, Dolce Gabanna, and a lot more. They also own retail brands like LensCrafters and Sears Optical.
561. There has been an increase in the life expectancy of people with Down syndrome from twenty five years in 1983 to sixty years today.
562. The word "Schadenfreude" in German translates to "pleasure from seeing others fail or suffer misfortune."
563. Anke Damask, a German fashion designer, creates clothing out of sour milk. After extracting the strands of protein from the milk, she then spins the fiber into yarn. She uses a type of big noodle machine to mix the ingredients together and it spits out textile fibers from the nozzle at the end.
564. From 2010 to 2015, the sodium content of thirty three Taco Bell menu items was secretly reduced by the company by 33% and nobody noticed.
565. The oldest and most difficult pasta to make is Italian pasta su filindeu, also called "The Threads of God." The recipe is 300

years old and only three women know how to make it in the remote town of Nuoro, on the island of Sardinia.
566. Just as we have leap years in our calendar we also have leap seconds that are added every few years to adjust for Earth's speed of rotation.
567. In honor of Roman dictator Julius Caesar, the month of July was named after him. He actually helped develop the Julian calendar, which is the precursor to the Gregorian calendar that we use today.
568. The longest solar eclipse in the 21st century lasted six minutes and thirty nine seconds. The next time another solar eclipse surpasses it in duration will be on June 13, 2132.
569. In the Czech Republic, there is a church made entirely of bones called the Sedlec Ossuary, featuring a collection of dismembered and bleached human remains. It contains the remains of between 40,000 and 70,000 people, a lot of whom died during the plague in 1418 and during the Hussite Wars of the 15th century. It's located under the cemetery church of "All Saints" and has a variety of objects such as candelabras, candle holders, and chalices made from bones.
570. The original design for Mount Rushmore was to carve the four presidents from the waist up, but the lack of funding made the carver stop after the faces were completed.
571. France has so many castles that some of them are up for sale cheaper than two-bedroom apartments in big cities like New York and Sydney.
572. Officially, Harvard is free for those with less than $65,000 in annual family income.
573. In Singapore, it's illegal not to flush the toilet. If you forget to flush it, you will be fined $150. It's even known that police officers do check.
574. The Spanish town of Huescar declared war on Denmark in 1809, then forgot about it for 172 years. During that time, not a single shot was fired and no one was killed. A peace treaty was finally signed in 1981 when a historian found the official declaration and realized that the war was still running.
575. Sphenopalatine ganglioneuralgia is the scientific term for brain

freeze. It happens because the cold dilates arteries causing a sudden rush of blood to the brain, which raises the pressure and causes pain.

576. There is a giant American wasp that has a sting so painful that the best thing to do if you're stung is to lie down and scream to avoid further injury.
577. In Lexington, Kentucky, residents can pay parking tickets with canned food donations during the holiday season.
578. Nikola Tesla, the Serbian physicist, engineer, and inventor, died penniless and living in a small hotel room in New York City. He had a terrible case of OCD and had some peculiar patterns. He became fixated on pigeons, he had to have eighteen napkins during every meal, and he would count his steps wherever he walked.
579. On March 27, 1973, actor Marlon Brando declined the Academy Award for best actor in his performance in "The Godfather" film. Native American actress Sacheen Littlefeather went in Brando's place. According to her, Marlon would not accept the award as he was protesting Hollywood's portrayal of Native Americans in the movie.
580. "Penguin One" is a chemical compound that received its name because of the fact that its molecular structure looks like a penguin.
581. A man named Seth Horvits accidentally received a military assault rifle when he ordered a TV from Amazon in 2012.
582. A contest in 1948, called the "Chicken of Tomorrow," was created to develop a superior chicken for its meat. The winner of that contest is most of the chicken we eat today due to its superior genetics.
583. The children's ring game known as "Ring around the Rosie" makes reference to the Great Plague of London, back in 1665. It refers to the rosy red rash in the shape of a ring that someone with the plague would develop. The pocket full of posie refers to the fact that people filled their pockets and pouches with sweet-smelling herbs or posies, as it was believed that the disease was transmitted via bad smells. And the ashes refer to the cremation of the dead bodies.

584. Residents of the village of Shitterton in England, tired of people stealing the sign of the village name, placed a one and a half ton block of stone with the name inscribed upon it.
585. Even though the UK call it football, the term soccer came from Britain in the 1800's.
586. The maximum lifespan of an olm salamander is over a hundred years.
587. The term "bug" for computers began because there was an actual bug inside a computer in 1947, when a moth short-circuited a computer on the US Navy.
588. Every six years hurricane names are recycled, except for those hurricanes that have been so deadly and costly whose names are no longer reused.
589. If there was a way to just harness .1% of the energy of the oceans tides, we would have enough energy for the current demand of the globe five times over.
590. In April of 2016, a seventeen year old girl in India had a 2.2 pound (one kilogram) hairball removed from her stomach after she had been regularly chewing on her hair for five years.
591. In order to protect their eyes from blowing sand, camels are equipped with three eyelids. The upper and lower eyelids have eyelashes; the third one is a thin membrane that they can see through even in a sandstorm.
592. The biggest tire graveyard of the world is located in Sulaibiya, Kuwait. Every year, enormous holes are dug into the desert and filled with old tires. There are more than seven million tires there already. In fact, the dump is so large that it's actually visible from space.
593. In July of 2016, in Prince Edward Island, Canada, monks went all around the island and bought up to 600 pounds (272 kilograms) of lobsters and then released them back into the ocean. The purpose of their action was to cultivate compassion for the lobsters and for all beings.
594. Mr. Stubbs, an alligator in Arizona, had his tail bitten off by a bigger alligator, so he had a prosthetic tail made out of silicone rubber that attaches to his back legs with nylon straps.
595. The size of a frog's tongue is almost a third of the length of its

entire body. If humans had the same sized tongues, they would reach the belly button.

596. In Thailand, people are not allowed to have over 120 playing cards thanks to a 1935 law known as the Playing Cards Act. Anti-gambling laws in Thailand are quite strict. Virtually all forms of gambling are banned.

597. Tuna imported to the US from Thailand is up to 40% illegal or unreported, followed by 45% of pollock imports from China, and 70% of salmon imports.

598. Kimagayo, the Japanese anthem, is the shortest national anthem in the world by text length, consisting of only thirty two Japanese alphabetical characters and only eleven bars of music in length.

599. In Peaks Island, Maine, there is a museum entirely dedicated to umbrella sleeves. There are over 700 umbrella coverings that hang from the walls and ceiling.

600. In China, there are parking spots designated just for women drivers that are 50% larger than normal spaces. Additionally, they are outlined in pink and have ladies' bathroom style symbols on them.

601. Whale milk contains a high percentage of fat which makes it very thick. In fact, it has the same consistency of toothpaste. The high fat content not only helps nourish the whale calf, but it also prevents the milk from dissolving in the water.

602. The first autonomous, untethered, and entirely soft robot has been created by researchers at Harvard University. It is a small, 3-D printed robot and it was nicknamed Octobot.

603. The best selling beer in America is Bud Lite, followed by Coors Lite, and then regular Budweiser.

604. The name of the fictional character James Bond was taken by author Ian Fleming from American ornithologist James Bond, a Caribbean bird expert and author of the Field Guide Birds of the West Indies.

605. In 1971, the first email ever was sent by computer engineer Ray Tomlinson. He sent messages to himself from one machine to the other.

606. As part of the training program, all US astronauts are required

to learn Russian. This is because they have to be able to run the International Space Station using Russian language training manuals if necessary.
607. In the 1980's, in an attempt to save some money, the head of American Airlines at the time, Robert Crandall, decided to remove a single olive from each salad served in first class. It saved them $40,000 that year.
608. It's possible to die from drowning twenty four hours after leaving water. It's known as dry drowning and the victims can be walking and talking while their lungs are actually filled with water.
609. In 2016, Nike created self-lacing shoes similar to the ones in the movie "Back To The Future."
610. "Skeletons in the Closet" is the name of a gift shop at the Los Angeles County Coroner's Office.
611. Buzkashi is the national sport of Afghanistan. It consists of a headless carcass of a calf or goat that is kept in the center of a field while two opposing teams on horseback try to get hold of the carcass and carry it to the goal area. The game can sometimes last for days.
612. Kangaroos cannot move backwards due to their appendages which impede them to move in reverse. However, their muscular legs, big feet, and tails are a great combination for them to move forward and hop effectively.
613. A Malaysian man named Ho Eng Hui, nickname "Master Ho," holds the world record for piercing four coconuts with a bare finger within just 12.1 seconds during an event that took place on April 21, 2011, in the city of Milan in Italy.
614. Professor Charles Gerba of The University of Arizona's Department of Soil, Water, and Environmental Science states that about 20% of office coffee mugs carry fecal bacteria.
615. Monkeys have been trained by researchers to recognize themselves in mirrors. One of the first things they did when being in front of the mirror was to check out all the places on their bodies that they have never seen before, especially their genitalia area. Monkeys were contorting and spreading their

legs in front of the mirror to get a better look at all unseen corners of their bodies.

616. In Ribeauville, France, bees started producing honey in different shades of blue and green. Further studies by beekeepers later revealed that instead of collecting nectar from flowers, the bees were feeding on remnants of colored M&M candy shells that were being processed by a plant located 2.5 miles (four kilometers) away.

617. In "Green Eggs and Ham," Dr. Seuss best-selling book, there is only one word with more than one syllable, which is the word "anywhere." The book was actually written as the result of a bet, where he was challenged to write a book using just fifty words.

618. The act of "fubbing" or "phone snubbing" is becoming a very real epidemic among Americans according to new research published in the Journal of Computers and Human Behavior. Fubbing is the act of snubbing someone in a social situation by looking down at the phone instead of paying attention to them; this behavior can affect and damage relationships, even leading to severe depression and lower rates of life satisfaction.

619. Humans have a gene called the "Sonic Hedgehog gene." It was first discovered in the fruit fly and is named for the spiky appearance of fruit fly larvae that have mutated versions of the gene. The name Sonic was given by British student Robert Riddle who took it from a British comic book of his daughters.

620. It took over twenty two years to build the Taj Mahal in India. Construction began in 1632 and finished in 1653. It was built by Emperor Shah Jahan, who was in deep grief over his passing wife, as a tribute to their love.

621. For thousands of years the Mayans have cultivated central American stingless bees even keeping them as pets around their home. Some of the hives have been recorded to last over eighty years, being passed down from generation to generation.

622. Cheese making artists at Dublin Science Gallery made cheese using bacteria from several artists and scientists. The bacteria were collected using sterile cotton swabs from different parts of their body including the belly button, mouth, and even tears.

623. Up until the 1990's, the halftime show at the Super Bowl was just a break that included marching bands and drill teams. The intention was to simply fill in the time so that fans and TV viewers could go to the concession stand, get snacks, or just go to the bathroom.
624. Hawaii is the only American state that is not geographically located in North America, the only one to be entirely surrounded by water, and the only one that does not have a straight line as a boundary.
625. After 9/11, the Kenyan Masai gave the United States fourteen blessed cows as a show of sympathy. Cows are considered to be sacred for them and are actually valued above all possessions.
626. The Apple desktop interface was inspired by the company Xerox.
627. Rhinorrhea is the medical term for a runny nose.
628. According to Vincent van Gogh's brother, his last words were: "The sadness will last forever."
629. In Marino, Italy, there is a McDonald's where you can have your meal and also check out an ancient Roman road at the same time. The road was actually built between the second and first centuries B.C., but it was only discovered when the McDonald's was being built, in 2014. The road was excavated, documented, and enclosed in a gallery with a glass roof so that customers can look down on it.
630. Contrary to most people's belief, there is no lead in a pencil. Its core is made of a non-toxic mineral called graphite.
631. The Atlantic Ocean is significantly saltier than the Pacific Ocean.
632. According to a study conducted at Harvard and published in the New York Times, if you were born on September 16, you share a birthday with more people than anyone who was born on a different date.
633. Unlike normal tattoos, braille tattoos are not made of ink, but instead are made of metal beads that are put under the skin to create designs of braille messages.
634. Kodinhi is a village in Kerala, India, with a high occurrence of multiple births. There are 2,000 families in the village and

around 200 pairs of twins. There is still no scientific explanation for this.

635. Fish have taste buds on their tongues, lips and bodies. Taste buds need moisture to work and because fish live in water all the time, taste buds can survive not only in the inside of their mouths, but also on the exterior skin of their flanks and fins.

636. Wu Hsia, from China, had an ex-girlfriend and current girlfriend jump off a bridge into a river; they wanted to see who he would rescue. He rescued his current girlfriend.

637. In the last thirty five years, the FedEx logo has won over forty design awards and was ranked as one of the eight best logos. The white arrow in the logo is crafted by blending two different fonts together and it was an intentional design choice.

638. When Poison Dart frogs are bred in captivity, they are completely non-toxic. In fact, wild caught frogs progressively lose their poisons in captivity. In order to create their toxins, they need certain chemicals that are present in the insects they eat in the wild. So when in captivity, they don't get the same insects as their food, hence they are no longer poisonous.

639. During the Afghanistan War, British Corporal Sean Jones ordered his men to affix bayonets to their guns and charge across 264 feet (eighty meters) of open ground against the Taliban forces as their men were ambushed, outnumbered, and under fire. It actually worked; enemy forces scattered fleeing the fight, due to the unexpected move.

640. The average lifespan of a human taste bud is seven to ten days. Human taste bud cells undergo continual turnover, even into adulthood.

641. According to a study done by PhD student Courtney Marneweck, at The School of Life Sciences at The University of KwaZulu-Natal in South Africa, rhinoceroses use communal defecation sites, meaning they poop together. The male rhinos can actually figure out how many other males are around and the reproductive state of female mates from this site.

642. McDonald's has its own university in Shanghai, China, called the Hamburger University. It trains students in restaurant management skills and has over 275,000 graduates. With a

selection rate of 1% at its campus, this intense week-long training program is more exclusive than Harvard.
643. In Saudi Arabia, all Starbucks coffee shops have a gender wall that separates single men from women and families.
644. Director David Fincher wanted Ben Affleck to wear a Yankees cap for a scene while filming "Gone Girl." Affleck, a huge fan of the Red Sox, refused. After a four day production halt, they finally came to an agreement that he would wear a Mets cap.
645. The spiciest chips in the world are the Carolina Reaper Madness chip. It is so spicy that it is sold as a single and comes in a coffin shaped package. The reaper pepper actually holds the Guinness World Record for the hottest chilli pepper on Earth, and the Carolina Reaper Madness chip is also seasoned with ghost peppers and chipotle seasoning.
646. In ancient China, seeing a spider dropping down from its web was a sign of good luck, even luckier if it was a white spider. People believed that they would be blessed with gifts and good luck from heaven.
647. The lampposts in New York City's Central Park have numbers on them to help people navigate in case they get lost. The first two or three numbers indicate the closest cross street, while the last number shows what side of town you are closest to. Additionally, an odd number means you are on the west side, while an even number means you are on the east.
648. If you could drive in a straight line to outer space, it would only take an hour to get there if you were going sixty miles (ninety kilometers) an hour.
649. On the average adult scalp, 115 feet (thirty five meters) of hair fiber is produced every day. On average, 90% of scalp hairs are growing while 10% are resting.
650. Research found in a study in 2015 showed that people use more of the DNA that's passed on from their fathers than their mothers.
651. The world record for the most bones broken in a lifetime is held by Evel Knievel, the pioneer of motorcycle long jumping exhibitions, who has suffered 433 fractured bones.

652. The first actor to appear on the cover of Time Magazine was Charlie Chaplin, on July 6, 1925.
653. The first police force in Australia was actually formed from the best-behaved convicts.
654. In Finland, mobile phone throwing is an actual sport.
655. A study published by Vegetarian Times concluded that 3.2% of US adults follow a vegetarian-based diet, which is about 3.7 million people.
656. Honduras and El Salvador actually went to war over soccer, on July 14, 1969. Although it only lasted one hundred hours, it took 6,000 lives and 12,000 people were injured.
657. The Japanese invented a pot known as the Kuru-Kuru Nabe which stirs the contents in the pot by itself when the water inside gets hot enough.
658. The shorter term for Canadian oil is canola, created by the Canadian Oil Industry in 1978. Originally, canola oil was called "the rapeseed oil," but the name resulted in negative connotations, hence the organization deciding to rename it.
659. Blind people tend to forget more memories than those who can see as they don't have visual imagery and can't look at photos to trigger old memories. There is a company named "Touchable Memories" that prints 3D objects from old pictures that help the blind touch, feel, and relive their cherished moments like never before.
660. There are some turtles that can breathe through their butts as well as their mouths, such as the Australian Fitzroy River turtle and the North American eastern painted turtle.
661. The movie "Straight Outta Compton" didn't exhibit in Compton because the city has no theaters.
662. There is a sport known as "archery tag" which is similar to dodgeball, however, foam-tipped arrows are shot instead of throwing foam balls.
663. Nodding your head in Albania means no and shaking your head means yes.
664. Fourteen year old Xiao Yun, from China, ran away from home and was missing for ten years, even thought to be dead. She was found at the age of twenty four living in an Internet cafe.

As she was good at the game Crossfire, other gamers paid to watch her play it. She slept at Internet cafes and public bath houses for a complete decade.

665. The snapping shrimp is able to regenerate its snapping claw. If they lose the snapping claw, the missing claw regenerates as a smaller claw, growing to become the new snapping claw.

666. The largest guitar in the world measures more than 42.6 feet (thirteen meters) long and sixteen feet (4.9 meters) wide, and weighs almost 2,253 pounds (1,023 kilograms). Although the strings are super thick, the same pitch is maintained as if it were a regular-sized guitar.

667. Found in Central and South Africa, the trap-jaw ant can snap its jaw shut at a speed of up to 145 miles (233 kilometers) per hour. To put that into perspective, that's 2,300 times faster than the blink of an eye.

668. There are some insects that don't have noses and use their genitalia to smell instead.

669. In 2015, the British government finally finished paying for World War I, almost one hundred years after the debt was issued.

670. Collingwood in Ontario, Canada, holds the world's largest Elvis festival, welcoming around 30,000 visitors every year. There is an Elvis impersonator competition and vendors sell Elvis memorabilia.

671. A normal pregnancy is about 280 days. In 1945, a twenty five year old woman named Beulah Hunter gave birth to a healthy baby girl after being pregnant for 375 days.

672. In order to protect the country's ports during World War II, the US Navy partnered with the mafia. For decades however, the US government has denied its collaboration and not just in relation to the Second World War.

673. The Empire State Building makes more money as an observation spot than it does from renting office space.

674. An album called "Wake Up" was released by Pope Francis in November of 2015. It features his speeches set to rock, pop, and Gregorian chants.

675. Queen Elizabeth and her husband, Prince Phillip, are actually relatives (they are third cousins).
676. If the entire globe's human population all came together into the Grand Canyon, we wouldn't be anywhere near close to filling it up.
677. Every two to four weeks, our entire outer layer of skin sheds. We actually shed at a rate of about 500 million cells a day. This is the major contributor to house dust.
678. The reason why the Sun and all the planets of the solar system are round is because the gravitational force of the planet's mass pulls all of its material towards the center, smoothing out any non-roundness.
679. Jimmy Connors beat Vitas Gerulatis in tennis sixteen times before he lost. When Vitas finally won, he said "Nobody beats Vitas Gerulaitis seventeen times in a row."
680. The Tapinoma Sessile, also known as the odorous house ant, smells like rotten coconut when their bodies are crushed.
681. The most common "how to" search on YouTube from 2012 to 2015 was how to kiss, followed by how to tie a tie, how to draw, and how to get a six pack in three minutes.
682. One barrel of wine contains around twenty five cases, or 300, twenty five ounces (750 millimeter) bottles of wine.
683. The average sloth travels only 123 feet (37.5 meters) per day. To put it into perspective, that is less than half the length of a football field.
684. A fifty six year old Indian woman named Kamla Devi was ambushed by a leopard. She actually managed to kill the animal with the only thing that she had on her: an iron sickle.
685. People on average blink about twelve times per minute. That's about 10,000 blinks on average per day.
686. There is an annual festival dedicated exclusively to Pikachu in Yokohama, Japan. The Pikachu outbreak is a week-long festival where crowds of dancing Pikachus, along with numerous statues, take over the entire city.
687. The first atomic bomb ever made was the gadget. It was successfully tested at Trinity Site, New Mexico, on July 16,

1945. The test code was named Trinity and it unleashed an explosion with the energy of about twenty kilotons of TNT.
688. On August 5, 1914, the first electric traffic light was installed on the corner of Euclid Avenue and East 105th street in Cleveland, Ohio. The design consisted of four pairs of red and green lights that served as stop and go indicators, each mounted on a corner post. It was created by James Hodge, who received a US patent for his municipal traffic control system.
689. Five hundred stormtroopers were placed on the Great Wall of China by Disney to promote Star Wars the Force Awakens.
690. From 2015 to 2018, there was a serial pooper that had pooped on at least nineteen cars that the police were on the lookout for. He was never caught and although he didn't cause any damage, he did leave a big mess.
691. Katherine Johnson was one of the most famous American mathematicians for her generation. Her fascination with counting allowed her to skip ahead in high school at the age of ten, and in 1961, she calculated the trajectory of NASA's first trip into space, and was correct.
692. Gobekli Tepe is thought to be the world's oldest temple. Located in Turkey, it was built 6,000 years before Stonehenge, even before the invention of the wheel.
693. The actor who played the creepy little kid in "The Shining," Danny Lloyd, stopped his acting career as he grew up and went on to actually become a professor, teaching biology in Louisville.
694. During exams, Internet black-outs have been imposed by governments in Iraq and India as a way to prevent students from cheating.
695. The jump in Mexican jumping beans originates from a moth larva inside the pod that twitches when abruptly warmed.
696. "Oo-ko" is the name of a straw goat that Santa rides on in Finland.
697. Dolly Parton, the famous country singer, is Miley Cyrus' Godmother.
698. Surprisingly, Abraham Lincoln was in the National Wrestling Hall of Fame. He had a remarkable physical size at six foot

four (1.95 meters) and he was widely known for his wrestling skills; in twelve years, he had only one reported defeat.

699. To cut down on their delivery time for products, Apple flies their stock first class instead of shipping it.

700. A study published in the Journal of Science demonstrated that lizards' sleep patterns are very similar to humans'. Researchers put electrodes on five lizards' brains while sleeping. The results showed that they to go through slow wave sleep, sharp waves, ripples, and rapid eye movement, or REM sleep.

701. Based on a study published in the Journal of Chemosensory Perception in 2012, people who scored high on a test for psychopathy had more issues for telling and identifying different smells. In other words, if you have impaired smell, there are chances you could be a psychopath.

702. A French enlightenment writer named Voltaire lived near country borders during the end of his life so that he could make an easy escape to other countries if his writings didn't please authorities.

703. Feeling chills while listening to music is the result of your brain releasing dopamine, a chemical that motivates you and makes you feel good while you anticipate the peak moment in that song.

704. The head designer at Apple, Jonathan Ive, was responsible for the products such as iMax, iPhone and iPod. He also helped designed the character EVE from the movie Wall-E.

705. The reason why flamingos are pink is because the algae and crustaceans like shrimp and prawns that they eat contain pigments called carotenoids. Their liver works to break down the carotenoids into pink and orange pigment molecules that get deposited in their feathers, bill, and legs.

706. If you go to the website Freerice.com, you can answer multiple choice questions and have ten grains of rice donated to charity for every right question you answer.

707 In December of 2016, a warning to motorists was issued by the Alberta parks system in Canada because there was an aggressive moose going around licking the sides of cars for salt.

708. In 1957, a convoy of five B-52 fighter jets from the United

States flew around the earth as a way to prove that they could drop a nuclear bomb anywhere. The convoy traveled more than 40,000 kilometers (24,840 miles) without landing to refuel, during forty five hours and nineteen minutes. It was called Operation Power Flite.

709. In the Rugrats movie, Rapper Busta Rhymes actually voiced Reptar.
710. According to a study done by researchers from the University de Montreal and published in The Journal of Neurolinguistics, bilingual brains are more efficient, and may be able to stave off symptoms of aging and dementia, in comparison to those people who aren't bilingual.
711. The gelatin that is produced as the result of boiling the bones, skin, and hides of animals such as cows and pigs is actually used to make Jell-O. In fact, people have been eating it since 1897 and it accounts for about 80% of the gelatin market.
712. A lady named Elvita Adams was saved by a gust of wind when she tried to commit suicide from the 86th floor of the Empire State Building. The strong wind blew her back onto the ledge of the 85th floor.
713. The largest library in the world is the Library of Congress. There are over 838 miles (1,348 kilometers) of bookshelves with more than 162 million items, including more than 38 million books and print materials, 3.6 million recordings, 14 million photos, 5.5 million maps, 7.1 million pieces of sheet music, and 70 million manuscripts.
714. In 1932, M&M Mars invented the original Three Musketeers candy bar in the United States. It was originally packaged as three individual mini bars of chocolate, vanilla, and strawberry nougat; hence the name.
715. The artist who painted American Gothic, Grant Wood, used his sister Nan and his dentist Dr. Byron McKeeby as his models. The house actually exists in Eldon, Iowa.
716. Mr. Splashy Pants is a humpback whale that has been tracked by Greenpeace since 2008.
717. In Jerusalem's Valero Square, there are some self-inflating giant flowers where pedestrians can stop for some rest. Installed by

HQ architects in 2014, these thirty by thirty inch (nine by nine meter) flowers bloom when someone approaches or when a tram is about to arrive.

718. Usain Bolt, known for being the fastest man on Earth, has a condition called scoliosis, which creates a curvature of the spine and gets worse as the body ages and grows.

719. In the state of Maryland in the US, there are no natural lakes. All lakes found there are man-made by damming rivers.

720. Approximately 50.6 pounds (twenty three kilograms) of manure are produced by a 1,000 pound (454 kilogram) horse per day, which equals to 19,900 pounds (9,000 kilograms) of manure per year.

721. The world record for the most medals won at a single summer Olympic Games is held by the United States. At the 1904 Olympics, which took place in St. Louis, Missouri, they won seventy eight gold medals, eight two silver medals, and seventy nine bronze ones, for a total of 239.

722. The only country in the history of the modern world to gain independence against its own will is Singapore.

723. "Bunyadi" is a clothing optional restaurant located in London, England. It costs up to $95 a person for food and drinks; you can choose between clothed or naked and pure seating areas where you will be served by semi-nude staff.

724. In the 1970's, famous true crime author Anne Rule once worked at a suicide hotline crisis center with serial killer Ted Bundy. Later she wrote a book about it called "The Stranger Beside Me."

725. According to the annual ranking of the best global brands generated by the management firm Interbrand, in 2016 Apple was number one for the fourth year in a row, with a brand value of $178 billion, and Google was number two with a brand value of $133 billion.

726. The ashes of actress Carrie Fisher, known as Princess Leia from the Star Wars franchise, were placed in a gigantic Prozac pill urn. During her life, she openly battled with drug addiction and suffered from mental disorder. The urn was actually purchased by Carrie herself; it was an antique porcelain pill

from the 1950's, and was one of her favorite prized possessions.
727. 8% of all global manufactured salt is used for de-icing roads, while only 6% goes for human consumption.
728. Some studies show that children will eat as much sugar as you give them because they're biologically wired to crave high-calorie foods during rapid growth. Until they are about sixteen, their bones stop growing, and that's when they start thinking of food as "too sweet."
729. In 1859, English settler Thomas Austin released twenty four rabbits onto his property in Australia; he thought that the introduction of a few rabbits could provide a touch of home in addition to a spot of hunting. By 1920, the rabbit population had reached ten billion.
730. The smallest adult of all time according to the Guinness World Records is Chandra Bahadur Dangi from Nepal. He was only 1.79 feet (0.54 meters) tall.
731. The flag erected on the moon after Apollo 11 landed on its surface was purchased at a local Sears store for $5.50.
732. In 2002, Daphne Soares from the University of Maryland conducted a study on American alligators. She found that these animals can orient themselves to the ripples created by a single drop of water, even in complete darkness. As their faces and bodies are covered with tiny bumps, they are far more sensitive than our own fingertips.
733. Based on population estimates released by the US Census Bureau in 2015, millennials aged eighteen to thirty four had surpassed baby boomers aged fifty one to sixty nine as the country's largest living generation, with 75.4 million millennials and 74.9 million baby boomers. Generation X, of ages thirty five to fifty, is projected to pass the boomers in population by 2028.
734. In our universe, there are 173 known moons. However, if we include dwarf planets that have objects orbiting them, the number increases to 182.
735. Seahorse babies have no stomach. Their digestive system has been described as inefficient, meaning that they must eat a lot

in order to stay properly nourished. A single seahorse baby can eat as much as 3,000 pieces of food a day.
736. Surprisingly, crocodiles have the ability to climb trees and do it regularly.
737. One of the loudest animals on the planet is the blue whale. They emit a series of pulses, groans, and moans that can be heard up to 994 miles (1,600 kilometers) away.
738. In the United States, 2016's Black Friday was a record breaking day for gun background checks. A total of 185,713 background checks were processed by the FBI, 400 more than the previous year. Black Friday is often the biggest day of the year for gun sales because of the huge discounts offered.
739. Ancient warriors used to use the monkshood plant to poison the water of their enemies. In addition, it was used as a popular werewolf detection tool; the flower was held under the alleged werewolf's chin, and if a yellow-tinged shadow appeared, that meant that that person was a werewolf.
740. George Washington asked his staff to wait two days after his death to bury him because he was so afraid of being buried alive.
741. A study done at the University of Edinburgh found out that those who smoke large amounts of cannabis in their lifetime have reduced bone density and are more prone to fractures.
742. In Japan, Bitcoin became a legal method of payment on April 1, 2017. It's only considered a method of payment however, and not a currency.
743. Vehicles without drivers cannot exceed sixty miles (ninety six kilometers) per hour in California. Companies who make autonomous cars, like Google, have the technology to make them go much faster, but must limit them based on the laws.
744. Besides being born on the same day and year, February 12, 1809, Charles Darwin and Abraham Lincoln had other things in common. They both loved Shakespeare, they both lost their mothers at an early age, and they were both abolitionists.
745. The first black woman to appear on the cover of the "Sports Illustrated" was supermodel Tyra Banks, in 1997.
746. Borborygmi is the name given to the grumbling you get in your

stomach. It's the result of the movement of gas within the intestines.
747. It is physically impossible for raindrops to form from pure water alone. At the very center of every single raindrop there is a mineral dust particle.
748. Originally Twinkie filling was banana-flavored. But during World War II, there was a banana shortage so vanilla became the standard flavor.
749. Antarctica has no time zone. Scientists who live there while doing research usually go by the time zone from their home land. In addition, daylight savings is useless, as most of the area experiences twenty four hours of sunlight during the summertime and twenty four hours of night during the winter. It's almost the same in the Arctic, although most of the North Pole is nothing but water and sea ice.
750. In Finland, there are more saunas than cars. Most countries in the world usually view a hop in sauna as a luxury, however, the Finnish consider their weekly sauna trip as a necessary right, up along with food, rye bread, and vodka.
751. It's possible to swim in beer at the Brewer's Starkenberger's Castle, in Austria. They have seven thirteen foot (four meter) pools filled with 42,000 pints of warm beer and some water. People can just sit and relax completely immersed. The beer is rich in vitamins and calcium and it's believed that sitting in it is good for the skin and can help cure open wounds and psoriasis.
752. A boy named Justus Uwayesu was an orphaned boy found living in a garbage dump by Red Cross workers when he was nine in Rwanda. He ended up going to Harvard on a full scholarship studying a Bachelor in Economics.
753. In the 1973 movie "The Exorcist," the green vomit that comes out of Regan, played by actress Linda Blair, was actually a combination of split pea soup and oatmeal.
754. The youngest individual winner of a Grammy is Country singer LeAnn Rimes. She was fourteen years old when she won her first two awards in 1997: "Best New Artist" and "Best Female Country Vocal Performance."
755. Szechuan peppers contain a molecule that makes your cells

touch receptors feel like they are being rapidly vibrated and give you that numb, tingly feeling.

756. In Amsterdam, there is a houseboat that works as a sanctuary for rescued cats. The houseboat has become a tourist attraction that receives about 4,500 visitors a year.

757. In the late 1990's, a vending machine that could automatically raise prices for drinks in hot weather was created and tested by the Coca Cola Company.

758. A lawyer from Kenya named Felix Kiprono, offered Barack and Michelle Obama seventy sheep, fifty cows, and thirty goats as a dowry for their daughter, Malia.

759. Oysters are born male, but they can switch their gender and become female when they want to lay eggs, and afterwards, they can either stay female or switch back to male.

760. The animal rights group PETA once suggested the band the "Pet Shop Boys" to change their name to "Rescue Shelter Boys," as a protest against the cruel conditions of many pet shops. Although Neil Tennant and Chris Lowe refused to change it, they did think that the request raised an issue worth talking about, as they mentioned in a post on their website,

761. According to the Guinness World Records, on May 31, 2014, 104 volunteers at the Deer Run Camping Resort in Gardners, Pennsylvania, made the largest smores ever, weighing 267 pounds (121 kilograms).

762. The least densely populated territory in the world is Greenland with only 0.6 people per square mile (0.02 people per square kilometer). In fact, the entire population is only about 56,000 people.

763. David Oliveira, a famous Portuguese artist, uses wire to draw in the air and creates sculptures that look like pencil sketches.

764. Cecil Chubb bought the Stonehenge for his wife for around ten thousand pounds in 1915, however, she didn't like it so he gave it back to Britain in 1918. Today it's worth approximately a hundred and fifteen million pounds.

765. The National Suicide Prevention Lifeline fielded the greatest number of calls in its history the day after Robin Williams committed suicide.

766. Paul McCartney's mother was a midwife in charge of the maternity ward at the Walton Hospital Liverpool. In fact, she had the privilege of giving birth to Paul in a private ward. Her ambition for her son was that he would become a doctor.

767. Jessica Cox from Sierra Vista, Arizona, became the first pilot ever to fly with no arms. She was born in 1983 without arms due to an unusual birth defect.

768. The largest living beings ever to have lived on Earth are the blue whales. Their tongues alone can weigh as much as an elephant and their hearts as much as a car.

769. USS Yorktown was the original name of the USS Enterprise. It was named after a World War II aircraft carrier.

770. Outside of Watson Lake, Yukon, there's a Sign Post Forest. It was started back in 1942 when a soldier named Carl K. Lindley was injured while working on the Alcan Highway. He was taken to the Army air station in Watson Lake to recover, and while he was there he was homesick, so he decided to place a sign of Danville, Illinois, his hometown. Tourists continued the practice and there are currently about 72,000 signs from around the world.

771. In Indian culture as well as other parts of the world, there are people who have taken a vow to never sit, lay, or squat for twelve years in order to transport their psyches into a realm of spiritual awareness not experienced by sitters; these people are known as standing babas. They stand before a small hammock in which to rest their arms during the day and torso at night. One of their legs must be on the ground at all times.

772. The brain of children triples in weight during their first three years of life and they establish about 1,000 trillion nerve connections.

773. Taco Bell's flagship restaurant in Las Vegas began allowing people in 2017 to get married inside the restaurant. They even installed a wedding chapel on the second floor for nuptials.

774. Apple Computers was actually founded by three people and not two, as it's usually believed. Ronald Wayne was the third co-founder, but shortly after the company's creation, he

decided to pull out, selling his 10% on April 12, 1976, for $800. Today that stake would be worth $62.93 billion.

775. Japan has a network of roads that can play music as you drive over them if you go at the correct speed.

776. One of the most venomous insects in the world is the Maricopa harvester ant. Twelve stings from such ants can kill a 4.4 pound (two kilogram) animal.

777. On March 29, 1867, 586,000 square miles (943,000 square kilometers) of land was bought by the United States at the northwestern tip of the North American continent from Russia, which is the current state of Alaska. They paid $7.2 million dollars, which equals to about two cents per acre.

778. There is an alternate Barbie doll with a regular nineteen year old's body. She's named the Lammily doll, has cellulite, brown hair, stretch marks, acne, and freckles.

779. In Japan, there is a preschool called "The Dai-Ichi Yochien" that has a courtyard that collects rainwater into a giant clean puddle. Kids assisting the preschool are allowed to stomp and splash around in.

780. In Tianducheng, China, there was a ghost town built in 2007 that looks just like Paris. It even includes a 354 foot (107 meter) replica of the Eiffel Tower. They have replicas of Italian, German, and English towns, but they are also deserted.

781. There are houses made within caves known as Yaodong in Northern China, where forty million people currently reside.

782. According to the joint-secretary of Nepal's Ministry of Tourism, novice climbers are not allowed to climb Mount Everest. In fact, climbers are required to have reached the peak of at least one 21,000 foot (6,500 meter) mountain in their lifetime in order to qualify to climb the mountain

783. In Herriman, Utah, there is a replica of Carl Fredricksen's flying house from the Disney Pixar movie "Up."

784. Based on a study conducted by a company called "Enigma" in February 2017, key brain regions are smaller in people with ADHD. These brain regions include the parts responsible for emotions, goal-directed action, learning, responding to stimuli, rewards, motivation, as well as memory.

785. The holly plant used as a decoration at Christmas time is known as the "Christ thorn" in Scandinavia. People there think that it represents the thorns that Jesus wore when he was crucified, and the berries are the drops of blood.
786. In May, 1991, the world record for the most people on a commercial aircraft was set when over a thousand Ethiopian Jews had to evacuate to Israel. The flight began with 1,086 passengers but ended up with 1,088 as two women were pregnant and had babies on board.
787. There was no one who was awarded the Nobel Peace Prize in 1948 as there wasn't a suitable candidate, but also because as a tribute to Mahatma Gandhi, who was assassinated that year.
788. There is a woman from Serbia named Bojana Danilovic who suffers from a rare brain condition called "Spatial Orientation Phenomenon." The condition causes her to see everything upside down, so she uses a special inverted computer screen and keyboard at work, as well as special work forms that are easier to fill upside down.
789. Mice can sing just like birds. It's just imperceptible to human ears.
790. Besides the Earth spinning on its axis, it also moves at a speed of about 66,900 miles (107,000 kilometers) an hour around the sun.
791. As of July 2011, more than one million observations have been made by the Hubble Space Telescope over the course of twenty one years, which have generated almost fifty terabytes of data. In fact, it produces over eighty gigabytes of data every month.
792. In order to impress a mate or to get away from a predator, octopuses can break off a limb when fighting. Some of them even eat their own arms once in a while, which some scientists believe may be due to a disease of some sort.
793. In Texas, possessing a pair of pliers is against the law.
794. Huy Fong Foods, the makers of sriracha hot sauce, chose a green cap for their bottle of sriracha to represent a fresh chilli stem.
795. In the rainforests of Southeast Asia, there are snakes that can fling themselves from trees and fly through the air. They can

adapt their body shape to generate the aerodynamic forces needed to fly.

796. Prairie dogs have their own complex language. They have different calls depending on the type of predator and they also make sentences that describe the predator.

797. In 2010, after the BP oil spill, Stephen Colbert stated that every time he said the word "bing," the Microsoft search engine would donate $2,500 to oil spill cleanup efforts. He managed to say "bing" forty times, raising $100,000 for the Colbert Nation Gulf of America fund.

798. Cheetah cubs have very long hairs that run from their neck all the way down to the base of their tail. It's called a mantle and it makes a cheetah cub look like a honey badger, protecting them from other animals like lions and hyenas.

799. Research in the UK for car accidents showed that short female drivers who sit close to the steering wheel are more likely to be injured an even killed if an airbag goes off.

800. The fear of belly buttons is called "omphalophobia." Sufferers of this tend to be afraid to have their belly buttons touched or to touch another person's belly button.

801. In England, Finland, Germany, and the US, there are playgrounds designed specifically for aging residents. They mainly consist of low-impact exercise equipment designed to promote balance and flexibility. Some of the machines include elliptical machines, static bikes, and flexors.

802. The author of the Harry Potter series, J.K. Rowling, also writes crime novels under the pen name of Robert Galbraith. "The Silkworm" and "Cuckoo's Calling" are some of the books that she has published under this pen name.

803. At the Guggenheim Museum, there's an eighteen karat gold fully functional toilet called America. Created by Italian artist Maurizio Cattelan, the toilet was installed in one of the museum's small single unit restrooms. Visitors are actually encouraged to use it.

804. "The Channel," also known as the "Tunnel" or "Chunnel," is a thirty one mile (fifty kilometer) long tunnel that connects the United Kingdom to Europe, located underneath the English

Channel. The trip underneath through the channel takes only about thirty minutes while an entire trip from London to Paris is only two hours and fifteen minutes.

805. The animators of "How to Train your Dragon" movie had to attend flight school in order to help them capture the realism of flying creatures soaring through the clouds.

806. The video game character Mario from the Super Mario Bros franchise was originally named Mr. Video. Later he was renamed as Mario after the owner of Nintendo's first warehouse Mario Segale. Meanwhile, Mario Segale earned himself the nickname of Mr. Video.

807. The most valuable company to ever exist was the Dutch East India Company in 1637. In today's world, it would be the equivalent of over seven trillion dollars.

808. During spring, when the weather is warm enough, adult muskox can shed up to 7.9 pounds (3.6 kilograms) of underfur.

809. Ayan Qurishi is a child genius who passed Microsoft's IT exam at the age of five, making him the youngest computer specialist in the world.

810. The world's largest gold crystal was found in Venezuela, years ago, according to scientists at Los Alamos National Laboratory's Lujan Neutron Scattering Center. It's the size of a golf ball, weighs half a pound (227 grams), and is estimated to be worth $1.5 million.

811. The US Department of Treasury Law forbids the use of portraits of living persons from appearing on government securities like money. Moreover, the portraits have to be of deceased people whose places in history are well-known by the American people.

812. In 2013, a group of footballers were caught being honest when they went into a convenience store that was left open and left cash on the counter for the items they took. The owner of the store was so shocked that he gave them all a fifty dollar gift voucher.

813. A bubble gum flavored broccoli was once created by McDonald's to get kids to eat more vegetables. However, testing

on children didn't go well; in fact, the candy flavored vegetable only caused confusion in the kids.

814. The reason why the hairs on your arms are short is because the cells that make them are programmed to stop growing every couple of months. The hair follicles on your head, on the contrary, are programmed to let your hair grow for years at a time.
815. In High Wycombe, UK, there is a tradition that dates back to medieval times where the mayor is weighed in full view of the public to see whether or not they have been getting fat at the taxpayers' expense.
816. From the closest point, Mars is 128,437,425 miles (206,655,816 kilometers) from the Sun and at its furthest, it's 154,845,701 miles (249,146,732 kilometers) away.
817. The prison's executioner in the state of Florida is an anonymous, private citizen who is paid $150 per execution.
818. In 2014, "CareerBuilder" did a study that showed that only 48% of Americans would quit their jobs if they won the lottery. Of those who said they would keep working, 77% stated that they would do it because they would be bored if they didn't work. Of them, 76% said work gives them a sense of purpose and accomplishment. Of them, 42% said that they would want financial security alongside the lottery win. Finally, 23% said that they would just miss their coworkers.
819. Before Super Bowl 51, Zoo Atlanta located in the Roger Williams Park Zoo in Providence, Rhode Island, made a bet that if their team lost, they would name a baby animal after the winning team's quarterback. That year, the New England Patriots beat the Atlanta Falcons; hence a Madagascar hissing cockroach was named Tom Brady by the Zoo staff.
820. The largest artery in the human body is the aorta. It's about the size of a garden hose.
821. The widest human mouth according to the Guinness World Records measures 6.7 inches (17 centimeters); it belongs to a man named Francisco Domingo Joaquim Chiquinho from Angola.
822. City street number seventy seven, in Reutlingen, Germany, is

the narrowest street in the world. It ranges from just 12.2 inches (thirty one centimeters) at its narrowest to 19.6 inches (fifty centimeters) at its widest. It was built in 1727.

823. Cinnamon was an ingredient used in embalming in ancient Egypt, as it preserved the dead.
824. In 1988, the steamboat Arabia that sank in 1856 was found under almost forty six feet (fourteen meters) of dirt in a field at a farm. Incredibly, many of the objects found were recovered and preserved so well that some of the food was still edible.
825. There is an Indonesian island where babies who die before growing their teeth are placed inside the trunk of a growing tree. The hole is then sealed and as the tree begins to heal, the child is believed to be absorbed. Within a single tree, there may even be dozens of babies inside.
826. In late February, 2017, Adolph Hitler's telephone was sold at auction in the United States for $243,000. It was recovered from the Fuhrer bunker and kept in a box at an English country house since 1945.
827. Being sarcastic is believed to enhance creativity in all parties involved in the conversation.
828. A woman in Florida spent six years of her life sitting on a couch. She died during surgery, when doctors tried to remove her skin grafted to the couch fabric.
829. The day after the terrorist attacks of 9/11, the British Queen broke tradition during the changing of the guard by having the guards play the Star-Spangled Banner. It was a way to show the UK's sympathy for the tragedy the US had to go through and for all those who lost their lives.
830. The average millennial is only worth roughly $17,600, and the main reason for this is high student loan debts.
831. Male kangaroos are able to jump as high as ten feet (three meters) and hop up to thirty seven miles (sixty kilometers) per hour.
832. Actor Tom Cruise is not as tall as you think. He is only 5.6 feet (1.7 meters) tall.
833. Daniella Perez, a woman who's in a wheelchair with no feet,

won a treadmill and a walk-in sauna in 2015 when she was a contestant on the Price is Right.

834. Tian Zi is a ten story hotel in Langfang, China, that is made up of three Chinese gods: Shou, the symbol of longevity; Fu, who stands for good luck; and Lu, who represents prosperity.

835. Off of the coast of Iceland, there is a natural rock formation that looks like a huge elephant.

836. Confidential data that leaked from the maritime industry revealed that a big container ship can emit the same amount of cancer and asthma-causing chemicals as fifty million cars. Based on this, the top fifteen largest container ships in the world may be emitting as much pollution as 760 million cars on earth all together.

837. During a basketball game, teenager Mick Jagger bit off the tip of his tongue when he collided with another player. From then on, he spoke and sang with a less posh accent and more of a street accent.

838. Steven Spielberg was rejected three times by the admission's officer when he applied for Cinematic Art school. When he was awarded his honorary doctorate from that school, he said he'd only accept it if it was personally signed by that admission's officer, which it was.

839. There is a US Navy research vessel designed to be capsized vertically. Most rooms there have two doors, one to use when the ship is horizontal and another when it's vertical.

840. Musician David Grohl was admitted into hospital after overdosing on a drug. That drug was caffeine. He consumed too much coffee while recording his new album.

841. Magician and escape artist Harry Houdini used to sell war bonds at the beginning of World War I, as well as teach American soldiers how to free themselves from German restraints.

842. In the Hocking Hills Welcome Center in Ohio, there is a Pencil Sharpener Museum. It features a collection of more than 3,400 pencil sharpeners that used to belong to Reverend Paul A. Johnson, who began collecting them in the late 1980's. There

are sharpeners of all kinds, from cars, planes, toys, Mickey Mouse, to even US presidents.
843. The only king in a pack of cards without a mustache is the King of Hearts. It's believed that the kings were all based on historical figures, such as Charlemagne and Alexander the Great. The King of Hearts is supposed to have been Charlemagne, despite the fact that he is often portrayed as having a full beard and mustache.
844. Owls have three eyelids. The upper lid closes when the owl blinks; the lower one closes when the owl sleeps; and the third one is a thin layer of tissue that closes diagonally from the inside-out, as a way to clean and protect the surface of its eye.
845. When Demi Lovato and Selena Gomez were kids, they both appeared on the TV show "Barney and Friends." In fact, the long-time friends were regularly shown together dancing and singing on screen.
846. There are no official duties concerning the role as the first lady, a position that is also unpaid. Despite this, many of them work hard to accomplish projects that they are passionate about and are notoriously targeted for appearance based criticism.
847. The original game of billiards was played on lawns outside. Then the game moved indoors to a wooden table with green cloth to simulate grass. That is why most pool tables are still covered with green felt.
848. During the Vietnam War, the external fuel tanks of the US fighter jets were dropped over Vietnam when they were empty or the pilot needed more maneuverability. A lot of these tanks were reused later by Vietnamese farmers as canoes.
849. Navid Azodi and Thomas Pryor, both University of Washington undergraduates, have created gloves that can convert sign language into spoken word via Bluetooth. They are called "SignAloud."
850. In the 1970's, people in Cambodia were murdered for being academics or for simply wearing glasses.
851. Sweety con Nutella is a Nutella burger sold by McDonald's in Italy. It consists of Nutella spread between a hamburger bun.
852. Pocho was a dying crocodile that was rescued by a man named

Chito. After recovering, the crocodile didn't leave and lives with Chito to this day.

853. Based on studies performed at The New York University School of Medicine, the higher up you are in altitude, the higher your risk of getting sunburned, with an increase of 60%.

854. Due to the lack of a liver enzyme, about 50% of Asians have trouble metabolizing alcohol, and as a result they end up with a red face when they drink, sometimes known as "asian flush."

855. Shamans in Mexico started using Coca-Cola for their rituals to heal worshippers. When Pepsi found out about this, they offered commission to Shamans to begin using Pepsi instead.

856. Based on the World Health Organization statistics, there were around 108 million people suffering from diabetes in the world in 1980. This number rose to 422 million in 2014.

857. The garfish or needlefish has greenish-blue-colored bones, which is caused by a pigment called biliverdin.

858. Martha Steward once dated Anthony Hopkins, but after watching "Silence of the Lambs," she broke up with him, as she was unable to avoid associating Hopkins with the character of Hannibal Lector.

859. For the third year in a row a restaurant called "Gaggan" has been crowned the best restaurant in Asia. The one page menu consists of twenty two emojis, each representing a different dish.

860. In the Pacific Ocean, off the coast of New Zealand, there is a 2,484 mile (4,000 kilometer) spacecraft cemetery where satellites and other spacecraft plunge back to Earth. The spot was selected because of how isolated it is from humans and shipping traffic. There are over 150 crafts in this cemetery.

861. To make egg yolks look more orange, marigolds and other plants that contain the pigment xanthophyll are added to chicken food.

862. According to the Farmer's Almanac, counting the chirps made by crickets can determine the temperature outside. So to convert cricket chirps to Celsius, you count the number of chirps in twenty five seconds, divide by three, and then add four to get the temperature.

863. The chewed end of a cigar smoked by Sir Winston Churchill sold at auction for £2,000. It was taken from his ashtray by a nurse who was looking after him while he was recuperating from a broken hip in Middlesex Hospital in 1962.
864. Lobsters have little urine nozzles under their eyes. When they fight or flirt with each other, they squirt urine at each other's faces.
865. The part of lightning that we can actually see, according to the National Severe Storms Laboratory, comes from the ground up, not the sky down.
866. Up until 1966, LSD or acid was legal in California.
867. Thomas Jefferson argued that the constitution should expire every nineteen years as one generation shouldn't have the power or right to bind the generation after.
868. In 2013, the Compassion in World Farming's Good Dairy award was given to Ben and Jerry's for their high quality treatment of their cows. They make sure that their cows get regular massages and their employees get double minimum wage.
869. Pig Beach is an island in the Bahamas populated entirely by pigs and it's possible for visitors to arrange a day to go swimming with them.
870. Before becoming an actor, Liam Neeson was a teacher and did it for a few years before he got fired. A fifteen year old boy pulled out a knife in class so he punched him in the face.
871. Glass is 100% recyclable and, in fact, can be recycled limitlessly without any loss in quality or purity. From every ton of glass that is recycled, over a ton of natural resources are actually saved.
872. In Los Angeles, there is a Santa Claus University that teaches professional Santa Claus skills such as toy knowledge, poses, and how to avoid a lawsuit. A great Santa Clause can make up to $100,000 a year.
873. Elephants are one of the few animals that can feel post traumatic stress disorder.
874. There is a condition called puppy pregnancy syndrome where

the sufferer believes that they are pregnant with puppies after being bitten by a dog.
875. The only continent that has no spiders is Antarctica.
876. About 35,000 year ago, the first ever sewing needles were made of bone by early humans. It's thought that bone needles were preferred over metal as a sewing tool because metal tended to rust and stain the fabric that it was used on.
877. In 2013, the Stockholm University Stress Research Institute in Sweden conducted a study that tested sensitivity to sounds immediately after a few minutes of artificially induced stress. It was found that stress makes exhausted women oversensitive to sounds. Even the normal decibel levels of a conversation can sometimes seem painfully loud to them.
878. Blowing your nose too hard, vomiting, or coughing excessively can actually cause your eyeball to pop out of its socket. It is known as exophthalmos and, if you are brave enough, you can just pop it back in.
879. Photographer Diana Kim from Hawaii had been documenting the homeless for ten years when she found her own father among them.
880. In 2015, nearly 12,000 gallstones were removed from a patient by Dr. Makhan Lala Saha, a gastrointestinal endosurgeon in India. They ranged up to five millimeters in size and it took his assistant four hours to count them.
881. A twelve year old boy was punched by Zach Braff for spraying fake paint on his Porsche as part of a prank on the show Punk'd. The scene had to be cut out.
882. The world's largest pig hairball is at Mount Angel Abbey Museum, in Oregon. The hairball is the size of a football.
883. The largest snail ever found according to the Guinness World Records weighed two pounds (0.9 kilograms) and measured 15.5 inches (39.3 centimeters) from snout to tail. It was found in Sierra Leone, in 1976, and it was named Gee Geronimo.
884. A Yale University study once found that one of the most recognizable scents to adults is the aroma of Crayola crayons. In fact, it ranked 18th, just ahead of coffee and peanut butter.
885. Bending trees intentionally used to be a way to mark trails by

Native American people. Some trees still remain today as hidden monuments.
886. Barack Obama personally thanked Japan in 2015 for karaoke, manga, anime, emojis. and karaoke.
887. The name salamander derives from the Greek word fire lizard. It came about when salamanders came running out of logs that had been thrown on a fire.
888. In the original Halloween movie, the mask that Michael Myers wore was actually a $2 mask of William Shatner from Star Trek. The mask was painted in white, the hair was teased, and the eye holes were reshaped.
889. In an effort to fight obesity, the government from Mexico City offers a free subway ticket to each person who does ten squats. Currently, 70% of the adult population is overweight.
890. At about nine meters underwater, your blood actually looks green because there is no red light under water, therefore, there is no red light that can bounce off of your blood into your eyes.
891. The Wieliczka Salt Mine in Poland is located more than 1,000 feet (305 meters) underground. It's one of the world's oldest salt mines still in operation, although the production of table salts was actually stopped in 2007. Over the course of the years, sculptures and even four chapels have been carved by miners, all made of salt. As salt mining slowed and then stopped, the chambers have been transformed into an incredible underground amusement park with grand halls, health spas, museum worthy art, and record setting spectacles.
892. A faraday cage was built into the ceiling of the Gin Tub in Brighton, England, to block cell phone reception. The owner wanted his customers to socialize the old-fashioned way by actually speaking to each other.
893. During the 2000 Australian Paralympics, the Spanish Paralympic basketball team was forced to give back the gold medals they won after finding out that almost all players were not disabled.
894. The popsicle was invented by accident by eleven year old Frank Epperson from the San Francisco Bay area, in 1905. He left his sugary soda powder that he mixed with water outside

overnight, and the next morning, it was frozen. He originally named it the Eppsicle, but the name was eventually changed to popsicle.
895. The fear of ferns is called pteridophobia.
896. The actor Don Johnson once asked famous journalist Hunter Thompson what the sound of a one handed clap sounded like. Thompson responded by reaching over and slapping Don over the head.
897. Jonah Hill wanted the role in "The Wolf of Wall Street" so bad that he accepted the position for only $60,000. For his role he received an Oscar nomination for the best supporting actor.
898. To locate and mark the locations of sea mines, the US Navy uses dolphins and sea lions. Dolphins have the most sophisticated sonar known to man while sea lions have exceptional low light vision and underwater directional hearing capabilities, which makes them the perfect animals for the job.
899. After playing World of Warcraft for three days straight, a Chinese avid computer gamer nicknamed Snowy actually died of fatigue in 2005. A service was held for her in a virtual cathedral inside the game, where over a hundred gamers visited her. In fact, she holds the Guinness World record for the most people at a virtual funeral.
900. Almost 5% of New Yorkers have a net worth of over a million dollars, which means one in twenty people in New York is a millionaire.
901. The town of Viganella, in Italy, does not get any direct sunlight for eighty three days during winter due to the surrounding mountains. Residents there have set up a giant, computer controlled mirror on the top of the mountainside to reflect the sun's rays onto the town.
902. At CIA headquarters in Langley, Virginia, there's a Starbucks where employees undergo an intense background check before they are hired. They're also not allowed to put customers' names on any of the cups. In fact, it's one of the busiest Starbucks in the country.
903. Norville "Shaggy" Rogers is actually Shaggy's full name in the Scooby-Doo cartoon.

904. Whisker stress is a feeling that cats can experience when eating or drinking out of a bowl that is too small. As whiskers are very sensitive to pressure, any time they come close to something, it triggers a sensation in your cat. If you see your cat trying to scoop out food with their paws, it might mean that they have whisker stress.
905. Someone has invented tea bags that look like goldfish swimming around in your mug.
906. Tear gas isn't actually gas, but a solid or liquid that gets turned into an aerosol. Today, the most commonly used tear gas is made of chilli pepper oil.
907. Lillico is a stray dog that walks up to eight miles (thirteen kilometers) every night to collect a food parcel that she returns and shares with her family, a dog, a cat, and a few chickens.
908. On the sidewalks of Boston there are poems that can only be seen when it rains. They were painted with special waterproof paint, which only appears when wet.
909. According to the EWG Shopper's Guide to Pesticides in Produce, strawberries have the highest concentration of pesticides with a single sample of strawberries that show twenty. On the contrary, sweet corn and avocados have the lowest.
910. "Keeping Up With the Kattarshians" is a real round the clock live streamed show where four kittens that are yet to be adopted and are living in a large dollhouse, are being filmed using GoPro cameras.
911. The average claw machine is only programmed to give the claw full strength every twenty tries.
912. "The ultimate" is the name given to the last thing on a list; "the penultimate" is the second last; and "the antepenultimate" is the third last.
913. The "Ilha da Queimada Grande," or "Snake Island," is an island in Brazil covered in deadly snakes, which remains untouched by humans. This reptile is responsible for 90% of snake bite related fatalities in Brazil and they're so dangerous that the Navy has forbidden anyone from landing there.
914. A man once hit his head while swimming in a shallow pool and

awoke with the ability of being able to play the piano skillfully after never having played any instruments before. This condition is a real thing known as Acquired Musical Savant Syndrome.

915. If you're a property owner in New York, you're able to request to have trees planted on your street for free, even choosing which species you want.

916. In June 2016, a leopard shark at the Reef HQ Great Barrier Reef Aquarium, in Australia, had a "virgin birth." Even though she hadn't had any contact with a male shark for years, she ended up laying forty one eggs; three of them hatched into healthy female pups. Virgin births are very rare but aren't unheard of in sharks.

917. In 1999, PETA conferred a humanitarian award to actor Steven Seagal for preventing the export of baby elephants from South Africa to Japan.

918. In 1937, Teflon was accidentally invented by twenty seven year old chemist Roy Plunkett, while he was trying to create a new type of Freon for use in fridges and air conditioners.

919. When the Nazis invaded Paris in 1940, French soldiers cut the elevator cables to the Eiffel Tower. They thought that if Hitler wanted to erect their flag on the top of the tower, they would have to climb hundreds of stairs to get there.

920. There are only two restaurant chains in the US that offer antibiotic-free meat: Panera and Chipotle.

921. Thirty nine members of the Heaven's Gate cult committed mass suicide on March 26, 1997. They believed that their souls would be transported to a space ship that was following the Hale Bob Comet.

922. The light on your microwave uses more electricity than it does to heat up your food.

923. Moon dust smells like spent gunpowder according to astronauts that have been to the moon.

924. More people die from sand castles than they do from sharks as people fall into holes that are dug up for building those sand castles than they are from being attacked by sharks.

925. There are between 100 and 400 billion stars within the Milky

Way. However, because our solar system is located roughly 27,000 light years away from the galactic center, we can only see about 2,500 of them at any point from Earth.
926. The traffic in London is so slow that it moves at the same speed as horse drawn carriages from over a hundred years ago.
927. Eating a late night snack before going to bed can cause you to have nightmares. When you eat, your metabolism is increased, so it signals the brain to become more active, which can result in scary dreams.
928. On May 8, 2010, actress Betty White hosted Saturday Night Live. She was eighty eight years old at the time, becoming the oldest person to host the show.
929. According to the Program Coordinator of the National Institute of Health's Human Microbiome Project, our bodies have enough bacteria to fill a large soup can. That is nearly five pounds (two kilograms) of bacteria.
930. A Doberman Pinscher named Khan saved a baby girl from a deadly king brown snake attack in 2007. The dog grabbed the girl by the diaper and fled her to safety, taking a venomous bite to the paw in her place.
931. In 1965, artist Salvador Dali drew a picture of Jesus on the cross and donated it to Rikers Island prison in New York. It hung in the dining hall of the prison for sixteen years, but then it was moved to a Plexiglas case in the lobby because prison administration feared that the prisoners might damage the painting. Surprisingly, it was actually stolen by four prison officials, including a deputy, in 2003.
932. There is a rare bioluminescent sea creature called the giant pyrosome that is made up of dozens of smaller creatures that reproduce through cloning. These animals are able to regenerate injured or missing body parts, and live particularly long lives.
933. In 2009, a new species of pitcher plant was found by scientists in the Philippines jungle, becoming the largest carnivorous plant ever discovered. It's called the se-pen-thes attenboroughii, named after Sir David Attenborough. Carnivorous plants

usually eat things like insects and spiders, but this one is so big that it actually eats rats.

934. Carbon black is a chemical used to make car tires, which gives them the black color. It's added to protect tires against ozone and UV damage. It significantly prolongs the life of any tire, and for this reason all tire manufacturers use it.

935. If you have an injury to your hand or fingers resulting in nerve damage, your fingers won't wrinkle when submerged in water.

936. Brooklyn College conducted a study which found that males are better at tracking quick moving objects while females excel at discriminating between different colors. This is due to evolutionary adaptation from our caveman days.

937. To date, a total of sixty three moons have been discovered that belong to planet Jupiter.

938. The 9/11 Living Memorial Plaza is a monument in Israel designed by Eliezer Weishoff. It's a thirty foot (nine meter) bronze American flag that forms the shape of a flame, representing the flames of the Twin Towers. Its base is made from melted steel from the wreckage of the original World Trade Center. There are plaques around the monument with the names of the victims of 9/11. It was completed in 2009, cost $2 million, and sits on a hill overlooking Jerusalem's largest cemetery.

939. The Milky Way is named the way it is due to the milky band on its edge that is made of millions of stars that shine incredibly brightly. The ancient Romans called it Via Lactea, translating to "a milky way."

940. When farting, the chemical compounds that we emit may vary depending on what we have eaten, and also varies from one person to another. Essentially, the typical breakdown of a fart is about 20-90% nitrogen, 0-50% hydrogen, 10-30% carbon dioxide, 0-10% oxygen, and 0-10% methane.

941. According to a soldier who was guarding Saddam Hussein after his capture in 2003, the only time he ever looked defeated was when someone brought him the wrong cereal.

942. Thomas Edison, the man who is credited with inventing the light bulb, was afraid of darkness.

943. A new species of frog was discovered by scientists in Costa Rica. They called it Diane's bare-hearted glass frog and it looks exactly like Jim Henson's Muppet, Kermit the Frog.
944. Snapchat founder Evan Spiegel's net worth was $1.5 billion at the age of only twenty four, making him the world's youngest billionaire at the time.
945. Based on a survey done by Boston University researchers, young people who consume Jell-O shots are more likely to get into fights after consuming alcohol. Researchers, however, do admit that more investigation needs to be done on this subject.
946. The fish odor syndrome is a genetic disease where a person excretes an excess of a chemical called TMA in their urine, sweat, and breath, causing them to smell like rotting fish. People who suffer from this have on average of two million sweat glands.
947. The number twenty three is used by Nissan in car racing. In Japanese, the number two translates to "ni" and the number three translates to "san", so twenty three translates into Nissan.
948. In 1980, music star Paul McCartney was arrested and then deported from Japan for trying to smuggle in nearly half a pound of marijuana in his baggage. In fact, he spent nine days in the Tokyo narcotics detention center.
949. In 1850, American Express was founded as a freight and valuables delivery service. Because the new company US Postal Service was unreliable at the time, and it only allowed shipment of letter-sized envelopes, the company saw a business opportunity to ship larger parcels. Later on, the company took a turn when it began to realize more profit from a sector of its customer base that included banks and other financial institutions.
950. In 2011, a team of hackers at MIT turned their Earth and Planetary Science Department building into a giant, multicolored, playable Tetris game. The operation took four years of planning and two months of effort, working every night from ten until five in the morning.
951. In Japan, snow monkeys entertain themselves by making snowballs.

952. The largest leatherback sea turtle ever found according to National Geographic was 8.5 feet (2.2 meters) long and weighed 2,019 pounds (916 kilograms).
953. There was a bear named Wojtek that fought in the Polish army during World War II. His name meant "he who enjoys war." He carried shells to the front line and was taught to salute; he became a mascot for the soldiers and even developed a habit for drinking beer and smoking cigarettes. He survived the war and lived the rest of his life in the Edinburgh Zoo.
954. In ancient times, Egyptians would treat toothaches by putting dead mice into the mouths of people. They also used to mash up dead mouse paste with other ingredients to treat patients with pain.
955. It is impossible for cats to move their jaw sideways or grind their teeth because their lower jaws are attached to their upper jaws.
956. A group of flamingos is called a flamboyance of flamingos. Other names to refer to them as a group are a stand, a colony, or a regiment.
957. Your body paralyzes itself when you fall asleep to stop you from acting out your dreams. Sometimes however this doesn't happen and is known as sleep paralysis.
958. Canadian currency has tactile marks on them that allow the blind and visually impaired to identify the bills by touch.
959. In February, 2017, a new dating app called "Hater" was released. It matches people based on their mutual dislikes. Some topics covered are Donald Trump, gluten-free, camping, marijuana, butt selfies, and Taylor Swift.
960. In the 1940's, planes were a lot more comfortable. The Boeing 377 Stratocruiser, for example, had reclined club chairs throughout the cabin that could adjust into a bed so that each passenger could sleep while on intercontinental flights.
961. McDonald's for the first time in over forty years closed more stores than it opened in 2015 in the United States.
962. The largest egg laid by the whale shark measured twelve inches (thirty one centimeters) long, five inches (fourteen centimeters) wide, and three inches (nine centimeters) thick.

963. 90% of US media, including TV, radio, and news, is owned by only six corporations: Disney, CBS, Viacom, Newscorp, GE, and Time Warner.
964. Former American president Richard Nixon gave up his Secret Service bodyguards in order to save money for the government, saving an estimated three million dollars.
965. In the 1960's, a new punctuation mark called the interrobang was made by the American Typers Association. It was a combination of a question mark and an exclamation mark, which was intended to be used at the end of an exclamatory rhetorical question, such as "what the heck."
966. The Japanese national anthem is only five lines long.
967. Crocodiles mainly live in salt or brackish water, while alligators prefer to live in freshwater habitats.
968. The author of the book "Fight Club" was embarrassed of his own work after he watched the film saying that it was so much better.
969. People in Australia are twenty times more likely to drown than be bitten by a shark. In other words, an Australian is significantly more likely to win the top prize in the lottery than being involved in a shark accident of any type.
970. In 2007, a German shepherd stray dog saved the life of Shannon Lorio after she crashed down an embankment and was thrown through the back window of her car. The dog came from the woods and pulled her by the collar off of the trunk, placing her on the road where she could be seen by passing drivers.
971. During the 1930's, the US was in short supply of fabric so the women started using flour sacks to make dresses. Flour mills began printing patterns and different colors onto them in response for more variety.
972. On April 1, 1996, Taco Bell created a marketing gimmick which was a hoax. The full page ad appeared in six major newspapers announcing that they had purchased the Liberty Bell to help the national debt. The ad went on to say that it would now be called Taco Liberty Bell.
973. According to US and European laws, travelers whose flight is

cancelled or delayed must be compensated by the air company. However, only a few of the eligible travelers ask for it.
974. In Japan it's possible to buy a pyramid-shaped watermelon. They can cost $500 each however.
975. Cold urticaria is the name given to a type of allergy produced by cold temperatures. It triggers hives, swelling, and itching. When being too severe, it can actually result in fainting, shock, or even death. It has no cure.
976. In 2004, Google anonymously posted math equations on billboards in Harvard Square and Silicon Valley. Those who solved them were led to a website with another equation; if the last equation was solved, they allowed you to submit your resume.
977. Samuel Morse began his career as an artist, however, abandoned this after his wife became sick and died while he was away on an art assignment. He ended up inventing a method to communicate long distances known as Morse Code.
978. Currently there are over six hundred billion lego parts that have been created since the inception of the company. That's approximately eighty pieces per person on the globe.
979. Based on research conducted by Dr. Scott Pitnick of Bowling Green State University in Ohio, the tiny fruit fly, known as Drosophila Bifurca, develops big testicles that make up almost 11% of its body weight in order to produce a great amount of sperm. They can even produce sperm that are more than twenty times the size of their own bodies.
980. The official national animal of Scotland is the unicorn. It was used in an earlier version of William the First's Scottish Code of Arms and, since then, it evolved into the respected symbol the country sees it as today.
981. According to a study conducted by National Geographic, the urge to travel in humans is caused by the same gene responsible for ADHD and thrill-seeking behavior.
982. Hippophobia is not the fear of hippos as it sounds but horses.
983. Given that the left lung shares the same space in our chest as the heart, it is slightly smaller than the right lung.
984. In 1928, the founder of the Kodak Company was so upset by

the different numbers of days in each month that he suggested that the company operated on a thirteen month year, where each month had exactly four weeks. They actually implemented it all the way up to 1989.

985. According to Netflix, in 2015 alone, their users streamed 42.5 billion hours of programming, which is an increase from the twenty nine billion hours of the previous year. As of 2020, there are 167 million subscribers worldwide.

986. Ovulation of giant female pandas occurs once a year during the spring, for a period of two to four days.

987. Tying a giraffe to a telephone pole or streetlamp is illegal in Atlanta, Georgia.

988. In 1992, a 100-tree swastika was found by locals from Zernikow, Germany, during an aerial survey. It was made up of a group of large trees only visible from the air and was almost 200 square feet (nineteen square meters). In autumn, the yellowing trees stand out against the surrounding evergreens. It's not known exactly who planted these trees, but apparently it was created during Hitler's peak in the 1930's.

989. For Pluto to orbit the Sun it takes 241 years due to it orbits at an average distance of 3.7 billion miles (5.95 billion kilometers) from the Sun, while Earth only orbits at 93 million miles (149 million kilometers).

990. A galactic year or cosmic year is the duration of a complete rotation of the Milky Way, which is about 200 million terrestrial years.

991. In ancient Rome, women used to dye their hair blond with pigeon dung. In Renaissance Venice, they used to dye it with horse urine.

992. Since 720 B.C., the Chinese have recorded solar eclipse sightings.

993. Tears of joy are your body's way of balancing out your emotions helping equalize your body.

994. The "Pigg-O-Stat" is a device that came out in the 1960's. It's used when radiologists need to safely immobilize babies and young children who can't or don't want to sit during an x-ray.

995. A report issued by Michael Gibson Light, a doctoral candidate

in the University of Arizona's School of Sociology, concluded that ramen noodles are now more popular than tobacco as currency in US penitentiaries centers.

996. When Rolling Stones bassist Bill Wyman was fifty two, he married eighteen year old Mandy Smith, but they got divorced after a year. Later, Bill's thirty year old son, Stephen, married Mandy's mother, aged forty six. If Bill and Mandy had remained married, Stephen would have been his father's father-in-law and his own grandpa.

997. In 1923, the original Hollywood sign was erected. It was placed there as an outdoor ad campaign for a suburban housing development called Hollywoodland. In 1949, the sign was restored and shortened to just Hollywood.

998. According to a study of surgical residents who participated in the Rosser Top Gun Laparoscopic Skills and Suturing Program, surgeons who played video games made 37% fewer errors than those who did not, and even completed the surgery 27% faster.

999. In Mexico City, there are special bins where you can put your dog poo in it and get free Wi-Fi in exchange. The more poo, the longer the free Wi-Fi.

1000. Canada geese generally nest in the same region that their parents did. In fact, they often nest in the same nest every year.

1001. Human brains are very similar to nuclear reactors in some ways. For example, they can cool down and heat up, and if your brain does overheat, you can experience a meltdown.

1002. In the Canary Islands, there is a restaurant called "El Diablo" where food is served with the geothermal heat from an actual volcano.

1003. The record for producing the world's longest pizza was set in Naples, Italy. It measured about 6,081 feet (1,854 meters) long and had about a hundred chefs working on it together for eleven hours. To make it, it took two tons of flour, 1.6 tons of tomatoes, a ton of cheese, and fifty two gallons (200 liters) of olive oil.

1004. Mahatma Gandhi was married at the age of thirteen to

another thirteen year old girl. They ended up being married for sixty two years.

1005. A Russian Soviet star, which is a highly revered symbol for communism in the country, was once vandalized by being painted to look like Patrick, the cartoon starfish from the kid's show Spongebob Squarepants.

1006. The only president of the United States to remain a lifelong bachelor was James Buchanan, the 15th president.

1007. "Extreme Kidnapping" is a company in Detroit where people pay up to $1,500 to get tied up and kidnapped just for fun.

1008. The longest word in the English language, according to the Oxford English Dictionary, is pneumonoultramicroscopicsilicovolcanokoniosis. It refers to a type of lung disease and the word itself is forty five letters long.

1009. In 2011, a maze was created by farmer Tom Pearcy from York, England, by carving two football-field sized portraits of Harry Potter into a corn field.

1010. Ganymede is Jupiter's largest moon; it has a saltwater ocean buried under ninety five miles (152 kilometers) of ice. Scientists believe that it's sixty miles (ninety six kilometers) thick, which is near ten times deeper than our oceans.

1011. Friggatriskaidekaphobia is the fear of Friday the 13th.

1012. In 2007, a curry dish was delivered from Wales in the UK to New York in the US at a price of $3900. The dinner order was placed by Kanye West. The dish itself only cost nineteen pounds and the rest was the delivery fee.

1013. People with dwarfism in ancient Egypt were regarded to have special powers and were treated like Gods, given the highest social positions.

1014. The "Toy Story" character Buzz Lightyear was actually named after astronaut Buzz Aldrin, the second astronaut to walk on the moon.

1015. The reality show "The Voice" not only shapes participants to become new singing stars, but also rejuvenates the careers of its celebrity judges.

1016. 156 people have been exonerated and freed from death row since 1973, according to the Death Penalty Information Center.

1017. The first Latin American country to ban hunting as a sport was Costa Rica, in 2012.

1018. In the movie "The Dark Knight Rises," the plane that crashed with the help of computer generated special effects actually did crash the next year, killing two people on board.

1019. The word "testify" derived from the Latin word for testicle. In ancient Rome, when two men took an oath of allegiance, they would hold each other's testicles; also men would hold their own testicles as a sign of truthfulness while bearing witness in a public forum.

1020. 15th century Romanian Vlad the Impaler, the cruel warlord who helped inspire Bram Stoker's 1897 vampire novel "Dracula," is actually one of Prince Charles' ancestor.

1021. In 2013, Shawn Mendes, the award-winning Canadian singer/songwriter, got his start performing covers of famous songs on the social media platform Vine. Today, he is considered one of the 100 Most Influential People in the World according to Time Magazine.

1022. The first country to ban plastic plates, cups, and utensils is France, with a law that will come into effect in 2020. The regulation is actually part of the country's energy transition for Green Growth Act, which is the same legislation that outlawed plastic bags in grocery stores and markets.

1023. In Japan, on Valentine's Day, it's actually women who do the gift giving. Men have the choice to reciprocate or not a month later, on "White Day."

1024. Twitter users have a limit of messages per day, which is 24,000 tweets and 1,000 direct messages.

1025. On average, a koala sleeps twenty hours a day.

1026. 29% of the total Earth's surface is occupied by land, 33% by desert, and 71% by oceans.

1027. A prickle is the term used to refer to a group of porcupines.

1028. The fear of developing a phobia or anxiety about showing symptoms of a phobia is called phobophobia.

1029. Ethan Couch, an American teenager, killed four pedestrians while driving drunk. Surprisingly, he was given no prison time after claiming affluenza, a mental illness for being too wealthy.

1030. The animated film "Sleeping Beauty" took several years to complete. Walt Disney even got bored of it at some point and actually redirected his energy into the creation of Disneyland. In fact, the iconic Sleeping Beauty's castle was built at the center of the park as promotion for the movie's eventual debut, which was four years later.

1031. There is a manufacturer called "Unifi," located in Greensboro, North Carolina, that recycles plastic bottles into polyester yarn to make t-shirts, shorts, or even graduation gowns. In fact, thousands of college students there have actually accepted diplomas while wearing these gowns.

1032. Florida-based company "Moon Express" has been given permission by the United States government for lunar landing, the first of several missions to visit the moon and harvest resources from it. It is the first time ever that the American government has approved a private company to land on the moon.

1033. The North American bison is the official mammal of the United States. After years of campaigning by conservationists, President Obama finally signed a National Bison Legacy Act into law in May of 2016. This is the first official mammal recognized by the federal government.

1034. Bowhead whales are considered as one of the longest-living mammals in the world. In 2007, a whale was caught off the Alaskan coast, having a thirty five inch long head of an explosive harpoon inserted deep in its neck. The projectile was manufactured in Massachusetts around 1890, which suggested that the whale survived a hunt over a century ago.

1035. The feeling of not finding joy in things that usually bring you joy is called anhedonia.

1036. A robot that picks up dog poop was designed by the University of Pennsylvania's GRASP Lab. It was named "POOP SCOOP," which stands for Perception of Offensive Products and Sensorized Control of Object Pickup. The robot is able to

find and remove 95% of offensive droppings at a rate of one a minute.
1037. Artist Heidi Hooper from Pennsylvania makes award-winning art out of dryer lint.
1038. The designer of the international biohazard symbol, Charles Baldwin, stated: "we wanted to create something that was memorable but meaningless, so that we could educate people as to what it means."
1039. Viewing all the pictures shared on Snapchat in the last hour alone would take you around ten years to complete.
1040. The female Tasmanian devil is able to have up to fifty jocys or pups in one litter. They all have to struggle to attach themselves to one of the four available teats in the mother's pouch. Those that don't attach to one don't survive.
1041. Herbert Hoover, the 31st president of the United States, gave his salary away to charities or as income supplements to his associates.
1042. The University of Bristol conducted a study in 2013 that showed that 75% of people who have the gene ABCC11 don't produce any underarm odor.
1043. The oldest wooden building in the world is the Pagoda, in Japan. It was built using trees from 600 AD.
1044. In 1984, the famed artist Bob Ross painted a grayscale landscape to show a colorblind man he met that everyone was able to paint.
1045. In China, people who are caught cheating on exams are banned from repeating the test for several years. Also, if someone is caught facilitating mass cheating or paying someone to take the test for them, they can be sent to prison for seven years.
1046. There is a way to send secure passwords through the human body instead of the air. The idea was actually devised by computer scientists and electrical engineers from the University of Washington. They use benign low frequency transmissions generated by fingerprint sensors in touch pads on devices.
1047. In 2009, three masked criminals unknowingly broke into Swedish actor Dolph Lundgren's home. The intruders tied the

actor up and then threatened his wife. But soon, they realized who owned the house when finding a family picture and immediately ran away.

1048. The lead singer of the black metal band "Hatebeak" is a parrot.

1049. "Red Vineyard at Arles" was the only painting sold by artist Vincent Van Gogh during his entire life.

1050. On July 3, 1999, the first perfect Pac-Man score of 3,333,360 was achieved by Billy Mitchel at the Fun Spot Family Fun Center in New Hampshire. He also held world records in Ms. Pac-Man, Donkey Kong, Donkey Kong Jr., Centipede, and Burger Time.

1051. There is now a complete new industry around the globe where students have their university papers and other work done by unemployed graduates and professors. The students don't get in trouble as the work isn't copied and done from scratch.

1052. Donald Trump's star on the Hollywood Walk of Fame has been vandalized several times in the past. The greatest one occurred in October of 2016, when a man named James Otis dressed up as a construction worker, set up construction cones and signs around Donald Trump's star, and took a sledgehammer to the star, destroying it completely.

1053. The swastika symbol was actually used by many other cultures throughout the past 3,000 years before the Nazis used it. It has represented life, Sun, power, strength, and good luck.

1054. In 2014, the American Psychological Association conducted a survey that revealed that the most stressed out people in America are millennials, which are people between the ages of eighteen and thirty five, parents with kids under eighteen, and low-income families. The survey determined that the main source of stress was money.

1055. Alfred Heineken created the "Heineken World Bottle" in 1963 in attempts to create a brick that can hold beer whilst also being used to build a house. The project never took off unfortunately, however you can still see a beer brick wall in two places; the Heineken estate and the Heineken museum.

1056. While breastfeeding, the baby gives germs to the mother so her immune system can respond and synthesize antibodies that are given back to the baby.

1057. In the late 1900's, Howard Hughes, an American business mogul, bought an entire casino named "Silver Slipper" so that he could get rid of the neon sign. Apparently the sign was visible from Hughes' bedroom and it was keeping him up at night.

1058. The Mickey Mouse brand has recognition of 97%, higher than that of Santa Claus.

1059. Artist Millie Brown from London creates art by swallowing dead soy milk in a mixture of colors and then vomiting it onto a white canvas.

1060. The Double Tree of Casorzo is a unique tree found near Piemonte, Italy. It's actually two trees in one, a cherry tree growing on top of a mulberry tree.

1061. There was a man named Malcolm Myatt who hasn't felt the emotion sadness since 2004 after he suffered from a stroke.

1062. Alex the parrot was the first animal to ask an existential question which was: "What color am I?" He found out he was grey.

1063. Barbara Millicent Roberts is actually Barbie's full name. Her inventor, Ruth Handler, created her back in 1959 and named her after her daughter Barbara. Ken also has a full name too, which is Ken Carson.

1064. In the 1990's, the movie Wayne's World was filmed in only thirty four days, extremely fast if compared to today where most movies take many months or even years to film.

1065. In 2002, a HIV-positive character was created by Sesame Workshop to be in the cast of the South African co-production of Sesame Street. The Muppet was a five year old female kid who contracted the disease through a tainted blood transfusion. The purpose of this was to promote tolerance and reduce the stigma associated with being positive with HIV/AIDS.

1066. Baby carrots are just regular carrots. They are cut and peeled to make those bite-sized pieces.

1067. The largest living structure on Earth is the Great Barrier Reef, located between the Queensland coast and the western edge of the Pacific Ocean. It spans more than 1,243 miles (2,000 kilometers) of islands and submerged reefs.

1068. During the Cold War, the United States used to send textbooks filled with violent images and militant Islamic teachings to Afghan schoolchildren, as covert attempts to spur resistance of the Soviet occupation.

1069. Up to 0.3 gallons (1.5 liters) of liquid can be held by the human stomach at any given time. When it's fully distended, it can also hold up to 16.91 cups of food, which is about fifty times the normal volume of the stomach.

1070. In Switzerland, there is a company that for $29,000 will name your baby for you.

1071. About 427 species of mammals, 1,300 species of birds, 378 species of reptiles, and more than 400 species of amphibians live in the Amazon rainforest.

1072. There is an extremely rare genetic disorder called dermatoglyphia in which people are born without fingerprints. People with this condition have entirely flat finger pads and they don't have the arching or looping ridges of fingerprints as other humans do.

1073. Californian artist Bin Dun creates art by taking photographs of people from the Vietnam War and with the help of sunlight and glass, prints them onto leaves and then casts them in resin.

1074. Saddam Hussein had the Quran transcribed by an Islamic calligrapher in his own blood during the 1990's. Over a two year period, he had over seven gallons (twenty eight litrs) of blood drawn.

1075. Some species of baby whales are born with hair, but they often lose it over the first several days or weeks of birth.

1076. A teen from Georgia was arrested for stealing a goat in 2015 after confessing he wanted to take a girl out, asking her "would she goat to prom with him."

1077. In 2008, the Coral Spring beach in Jamaica was actually stolen and the thieves were never caught. Massive amounts of sand were stolen until it basically wasn't a beach any more.

1078. Blind mothers are now able to have a three dimensional ultrasound of their unborn child printed to get a better sense of the image thanks to 3D printing.

1079. Musician Pharell Williams was fired from three different McDonald's stores when he was only seventeen for stealing nuggets and being lazy. Later on he created a jingle with Justin Timberlak called "I'm Lovin' It."

1080. In 1919, due to a Spanish flu outbreak, the Stanley Cup final in Seattle was canceled. It was the first time ever that the finals were canceled.

1081. A study showed that female servers who drew a little smiley face on the bill increased their tips by up to twenty percent.

1082. If the New York City subway system was laid end to end, it would stretch from New York City to Chicago, covering 661 miles (1,063 kilometers) of main track.

1083. The popular known Panama hats are actually made in Ecuador, not in Panama.

1084. People used to use moist bread to erase pencil marks before the invention of rubber erasers by Edward Nairne, in 1770. In fact, the invention was discovered by accident by Edward thinking that he had grabbed bread.

1085. The sackbut was the name originally given to the trombone.

1086. The place on earth where the most twins are born is Nigeria.

1087. An average of 257 gallons (972 liters) of urine is produced by the fin whale each day.

1088. Based on studies done by Dr. Norman Harden, a headache expert at the North Western University, from 5% to 10% of people never experience headaches or face pain in their entire lifetime.

1089. The fear of seeing, hearing, or writing poetry is called metrophobia.

1090. Beyonce was making about $4 per second in 2014.

1091. In the movie "Back to the Future," the time machine was meant to be a refrigerator, however, was changed to the car as the writers thought that kids would lock themselves in a fridge recreating the scene.

1092. The only iguana in the world that feeds underwater is the

Galapagos iguana. They are able to hold their breath for up to half an hour and dive up to 29.8 feet (9.1 meters).

1093. A new material stronger than grapheme was created by researchers from MIT. It's ten times stronger than steel, with only 5% of its density.

1094. The first occurrence of identical bird twins ever was reported in the emu.

1095. Isaac Newton predicted that the world would end in 2060.

1096. The world's tallest tree is located in California's Redwood National Park. It's a redwood tree named "Hyperion" and it's 379 feet (115 meters) tall.

1097. Susan Wojcicki, the current CEO of YouTube, rented her garage to Larry Page and Sergey Brin in 1998 when they were creating Google.

1098. Inakadate is a small village in Japan that has reinvented itself by creating rice paddy art. The style of art is created by combining grains of rice in variations to make amazing images.

1099. Bedbugs don't have wings so they can't fly or jump. However, they can live for months without food.

1100. In 2015, a military Disneyland park called "Patriot Park" was opened in Russia. All visitors, including children, can ride in tanks, shoot guns, and buy and sell military gear.

1101. Todu Yamanaka, the CEO of Japan Airlines, earns less than the pilots of the company, takes the bus in to work, and eats in the work cafeteria. He stated that others who seek money first will always fail.

1102. Storing bread in the fridge instead of at room temperature makes it go stale six times faster.

1103. Jason Lewis was the first person to circumnavigate around the globe purely by human power. His journey began in 1994 where he biked, rollerbladed, kayaked and pedaled from country to country, finally ending his trip thirteen years later in 2007.

1104. The US Air Force accidentally dropped two nuclear bombs in North Carolina in January, 1961, when a bomber broke in two mid flight. Luckily neither of the bombs went off. If they had,

they would've been more devastating than the Nagasaki and Hiroshima incidents combined.
1105. Grapefruit juice affects the activity of certain enzymes that are responsible for breaking down many prescription drugs. The fruit contains compounds that block the enzymes, reducing the enzyme's ability to break down the drug. In consequence, blood levels of the drug may rise, resulting in a risk of new or worsened side effects.
1106. Another name for hiccups is singultus.
1107. The world's largest cathedral is St. Peter's Basilica, in Vatican City. The structure is 610 feet (186 meters) in length, it has an inside area of more than 163,000 square feet (262,000 square meters), and the main dome is 446 feet (136 meters) high. The cathedral can accommodate 20,000 prayers at one time.
1108. Members of the British royal family had no surname before 1917, but only the name of the house or dynasty to which they belonged. In fact, kings and princes were known by the names of their countries that their families ruled.
1109. There is an asteroid named after actor Tom Hanks, as the "12818 Tom Hanks."
1110. Fifty four year old Cong Yan from Jilin, China, walked daily with an eighty eight pound (forty kilogram) rock balanced on his head in an attempt to get fit and lose weight.
1111. In Tennessee, it is against the law to sell bologna on Sunday.
1112. The male African lion uses its urine to mark and protect his territory. The area can be as big as 100 square miles (259 square kilometers).
1113. In London, there is a pool suspended between two apartment buildings with transparent sides and floors. You can swim from one building to the other side while enjoying a view of London through almost eight inches (twenty centimeters) of glass casing.
1114. If you put a tube of regular water and a tube of morphine water in a rat enclosure, the rat will always drink the drugged water until they die. However, if you give the rat ample space, games, and friends, the rat won't touch the drugged water, even if you try to trick it by swapping the water tubes.

1115. "The Scent of First Love" is a strawberry found in Japan that is white in color and has red seeds. They are sweeter and richer than usual and cost up to four dollars for one berry.
1116. There are killer whales living in captivity with dolphins that have learned their complex language, and have started using it with each other.
1117. A mega-asteroid of around thirty miles (forty eight kilometers) across hit the Earth in Australia 3.5 billion years ago, causing tsunamis and craters bigger than many US states.
1118. If there are any students who are feeling stressed and anxious in the University of Victoria's Law Library, they are able to rent a black labrador named Echo. You get him for thirty minutes and can take him for a walk or just give him pats.
1119. The hottest year ever recorded was 2016. Overall temperatures over the continents and oceans were thirty three degrees Fahrenheit (0.99 degrees Celsius) above the pre-industrial average.
1120. Doctors have a checklist with nineteen questions before they see a patient that has reduced deaths by more than 40%. Some of the questions include "do we have the right patient" and "what operation are we performing."
1121. In the 1990's, the King of Pop Michael Jackson wanted to play Spiderman so badly that he discussed purchasing Marvel Comics with Stan Lee. No agreement was made.
1122. The designer brand store Kate Spade was co-founded by David Spade's brother Andy, along with his wife Kate in New York.
1123. Ingvar Feodor Kamprad, the founder of IKEA, started to work when he was six years old, by selling matches. At the age of ten, he used to bike around the neighborhood selling Christmas decorations. Then at the age of seventeen, he was getting money from selling fish and pencils. Finally, after his father gave him a small sum of money for doing well in school, he started IKEA.
1124. The leading cause of death among children aged ten to nineteen is road traffic crashes.
1125. There are a series of sixty five feet (twenty meter) long concrete

arrows all the way from San Francisco to New York City, that were created to direct traffic in the air from the pre-digital era.

1126. The first son of a former President who became President himself was John Quincy Adams. George H.W. Bush and George W. Bush are the only other father-son Presidents.

1127. In 2016, a fried chicken scented candle was released by KFC.

1128. The best man has that name because historically they were the best with their sword. This was so he would be in close proximity if the bride tried to escape or if the family attempted to stop the wedding.

1129. In 1958, a giant sculpture of an atom called "The Atomium" was built by the World's Fair in Brussels, Belgium, to symbolize the atomic age. It's 335 feet (102 meters) tall and has nine fifty nine diameter foot (eighteen diameter meter) spheres attached by tubes.

1130. In 1948, farmer Cecil George Harris of Rosetown, Saskatchewan, wrote one of the most unique wills ever written. He scratched his will into the fender of a tractor that he was trapped under for ten hours during a heavy storm. His will read "In case I die in this mess, I leave all to my wife." He died that night from his injuries. A judge ordered that portion of the tractor to be cut off and it is now displayed under a piece of glass in the University of Saskatchewan Law library.

1131. While filming the movie "Apocalypse Now," the production cast design decided to use real bodies instead of fake ones. It was only when the odor became too strong that the rest of the cast found out about it.

1132. Canada and Denmark are in dispute over a territory called Hans Island. The military forces of both countries regularly visit the island and remove the other country's flag leaving a bottle of Danish schnapps or Canadian whiskey.

1133. At the Bronx Zoo, for a $10 donation, you can name a cockroach after your partner on Valentine's Day. The money collected goes to the Wildlife Conservation Society.

1134. According to a study conducted by university professors across America, bi-cultural people may change their personality when they switch languages because language unconsciously affects people's interpretation of events. For example, women speaking Spanish were seen as more independent and assertive than women speaking English in similar situations.

1135. According to the former US President Bill Clinton, the Netflix series "House of Cards" is 99% real.

1136. There are over 3,500 species of mosquitoes. They vary in sizes, appetites, and dispositions.

1137. In 1938, Adolph Hitler was named Man of the Year by Time Magazine.

1138. The Secretary Bird is a predator bird that kills its prey, mostly poisonous snakes and big lizards, by stomping on its head until it's either incapacitated or dead. Its kick packs a punch of up to 195 Newton, which is equal to roughly five times the body weight of the bird itself.

1139. There is a strain of seaweed that tastes like bacon when cooked that even has twice the nutritional value of kale, discovered by researchers at Oregon State.

1140. Mushrooms were considered the plant of immortality by ancient Egyptians. In fact, mushrooms were decreed food for royalty by the Pharaohs of Egypt, so no commoner could even touch them.

1141. In 1977, a surfing Santa fifteen cent Christmas stamp was designed by Roger Roberts, in Australia, which caused a lot of controversy and complaints from people around Australia. The drawing included a Santa Claus riding a surfboard to deliver presents.

1142. "Left Handers Day" is celebrated every year on August 13.

1143. In 2001, a study done by Diane Reese of the Osborn Laboratory of Marine Sciences at the New York Aquarium determined that dolphins actually recognize themselves when looking in a mirror; they also notice changes in their appearance. In previous studies, only higher primates such as humans and chimpanzees had demonstrated self-recognition in mirrors

1144. The maximum life sentence in Norway is only twenty one years, except for genocide in war crimes. Despite this, the nation has one of the lowest recidivism rates in the world at

20%. In contrast, the United States has one of the highest with 76.6% of prisoners rearrested within the following five years.

1145. In 2015, a man skipped out on his bill at a Houston restaurant and later was seen running into an empty building across the street. After arriving at the building, the police officers jokingly called out "Marco" to which the suspect accidentally replied "Polo." He was immediately detained.

1146. Before 1900, and according to the Cheetah Conservation Fund, the cheetah population was over 100,000. But from then on, the cheetah has gone extinct in over twenty countries, with only 7,100 cheetahs remaining worldwide.

1147. The only continent without at least one desert region is Europe. In order for an area to qualify as a desert, it must get less than ten inches (twenty five centimeters) of rain per year.

1148. Spiders cannot digest solid food. They need to turn their prey into a liquid form before actually eating them. To do so, they emanate digestive enzymes from their stomach onto the victim's body. Once the enzymes break down the tissues of the prey, they suck up the liquid remains.

1149. On June 1, 1923, Canada approved the Chinese Exclusion Act, which lasted until 1947. The law stopped Chinese immigration to Canada for almost a quarter of a century.

1150. In South Australia, it is against the law to disrupt a wedding or a funeral.

1151. Fruitarianism is a subgroup of veganism. The diet basically consists of fruit and possible nuts and seeds. In fact, there are some fruitarians that will only eat what would naturally fall from a plant.

1152. In the Northwestern Territories in Canada, license plates are shaped like polar bears.

1153. An Airbus 321 once made its way from Athens to Zurich carrying a stowaway Greek cat in the undercarriage. It had shock and hypothermia, but incredibly it survived.

1154. Inventor Alexander Graham Bell was given his middle name, Graham, when he was ten years old.

1155. In the days following September 11, around 36,000 units of blood were donated to the New York Blood Center by New

Yorkers willing to help. However, blood cannot be used more than a few weeks after donation, so unfortunately many units had to be discarded.
1156. The largest falcon hospital in the world is in Abu Dhabi, housing more than 6,000 falcons.
1157. In the year 1900, a new alarm mechanism was developed by inventor Ludwig Ederer. When the alarm went off, the bed rose to a forty five degree angle and tipped you out of bed.
1158. As of 2014, the Centers for Disease Control and Prevention, or the CDC, reported that one in sixty eight children, or more specifically, one in forty two boys and one in 189 girls has autism spectrum disorder, which includes a wide range of symptoms and skills in different levels of disability.
1159. In 1860, Valentine Tapley, a pike County farmer and loyal democrat, promised to never trim his beard again if Abraham Lincoln was elected president. He kept his word and his beard grew to 12.5 feet (3.8 meters) long.
1160. The Bullockornis was a prehistoric bird that grew up to 8.2 feet (2.5 meters) tall and weighed approximately 550.6 pounds (250 kilograms). It was nicknamed the demon duck of doom.
1161. The only confirmed person in history that has ever been hit by a meteorite is Anne Hodges from Alabama, US. On a clear day in November of 1954, a softball sized hunk of black rock broke through her ceiling, bounced off a radio, and hit her in the thigh while she was having a nap on her couch, leaving a pineapple shaped bruise.
1162. Torn bank notes in Australia are worth half of the proportion of the note left, so half of a $20 bill is actually $10.
1163. Although bison may look slow and not very agile, they can run at thirty five miles (fifty six kilometers) per hour and jump as high as six feet (1.8 meters) off the ground.
1164. There is a café in Bunkyo, Tokyo, called the Moomin House Cafe that offers coffee, treats, and companionship of huge stuffed animals. They will actually seat you with a stuffed animal if you want so that you don't have to dine alone.
1165. Newborn giraffes measure about six feet (1.83 meters) tall, making them taller than most humans.

1166. There is another variation of soccer where three teams face off against each other at the same time.
1167. It's known that elephants can favor one tusk over the other, making one shorter than the other.
1168. There are some whale species that go through menopause, such as the short-finned pilot whale and the orca or killer whale.
1169. The expression "paying through the nose" comes from Vikings times. It used to be a Viking punishment for those who refused to pay taxes which consisted of slitting the nose from tip to eyebrow.
1170. The average strawberry is covered by approximately 200 seeds.
1171. At the age of only twenty eight, Beethoven began losing his hearing, so he cut the legs off his piano and began sitting on the floor so he could compose music by feeling the vibrations.
1172. Cornell University researchers made the world's smallest guitar, which is about the size of a human blood cell. It was made from crystalline silicon and it has six strings, each about fifty nanometers wide.
1173. The world's first 3D printing restaurant is Food Ink. All the food, utensils, and furniture are actually produced through 3D printing. Using fresh and natural ingredients, the edible art is prepared by the finest chefs.
1174. Studies performed at Cornell University revealed that the tiger beetle runs so fast, it can no longer see where it's going. So in order to avoid obstacles, it has to use its antennae.
1175. Eyelashes' growth cycle is only three months, which is why they don't grow very long. About one to five fall out daily.
1176. Canine compulsive disorder, or CCD, is a condition that affects dogs that is characterized by excessive repetition of an action or behavior and can vary depending on the context. The condition is actually very similar to human compulsive disorders and is likely to be a coping mechanism for when the dog sees a situation as stressful.
1177. In 2006, a mummified human skeleton was placed on sale on eBay by a woman named Lynn Sterling, from Michigan, US. The online company removed the posting because it violated their policy against selling human remains.

1178. Ferrule is the name given to the metal band that joins the eraser to a pencil. It is also the name of the metal band at the end of a cane.
1179. There is a type of red banana that exists that tastes super sweet, creamy, and a little bit like raspberries.
1180. The world's largest floating bookstore/library is the "Logos Hope." A German charity organization operates it and it has over 6,000 books.
1181. Writer, actor, and comedian, Dan Akroyd suffers from Asperger, a form of autism. One of his symptoms is having an obsession with ghosts and law enforcement, which resulted into the idea of the "Ghostbusters" film.
1182. Children as young as five years old were used as chimney sweeps back in Victorian times. They were sent up the chimney to clean out soot and debris. Some chimneys were as narrow as twelve inches (30.4 centimeters), so if they got stuck, the master chimney sweeper would light a fire to encourage them to continue working. Shockingly, some of them couldn't make their way out and died of suffocation.
1183. John Tyler, Millard Fillmore, Andrew Johnson, and Chester A. Arthur served their entire terms as presidents of the United States without a vice president.
1184. There is a special daily wake-up call for spring breakers at the Holiday Inn resort in Panama City Beach, Florida. They blast "Circle of Life," Elton John's hit song from The Lion King musical, at their balconies every morning. The tradition began in 2012.
1185. In order to help her hatchlings emerge, the Nile crocodile rolls and squeezes her eggs in her mouth.
1186. On January 31, 1958, the first US satellite was launched into space. It was named Explorer I, it was about twice the size of a basketball, and only weighed thirty pounds (thirteen kilograms).
1187. The most valuable cow in the world, Missy, is worth $1.2 million. She produces 50% more milk than other cows and has superior genetics, making her embryos in high demand.
1188. When at war, the Philippines hang their flag upside down. In 2010, the flag was accidentally displayed upside down behind

its President when meeting with President Obama and other leaders of the Assembly of Southeast Asian nations. It caused great confusion and tension as everyone thought it was an act of war.
1189. Based on studies performed by researchers at the National Hansen's Disease Program in Baton Rouge, Louisiana, the armadillo is one of the few mammals that harbor the bacteria that cause leprosy.
1190. On average, five to seven adults are reported missing every day in Las Vegas.
1191. As a way to prevent hunched backs, Dutch designer Jeffrey Heiligers has created posture garments. After working with a physiotherapist to identify positions that cause back, neck, and shoulder pain, he created clothes that tighten slightly and become uncomfortable when the wearer slumps their shoulders.
1192. The first ever decree about human rights was issued by Persian king Cyrus the Great in 539 B.C. The decree established to free the slaves, declared that all people had the right to choose their own religion, and established racial equality.
1193. The NYPD has undercover cop cabs. Safe exchange zones have been created by some police stations; these zones are designated areas for trades arranged through Craigslist and similar sites.
1194. There is a hybrid sport called chess boxing that combines the mental battle of chess and the physical struggle of boxing. Performers have to learn how to balance their strategy on the chess board with the plan of attack in the boxing match.
1195. The band members of Good Charlotte were known to protest again KFC's treatment of chickens, however, after 2013 they appeared in several KFC commercials in Australia and even tried to set a new world record for eating KFC on Australia's got talent.
1196. There was a calendar made during the French Revolution known as the "French Republican Calendar" that had 100 seconds in a minute, ten hours in a day, ten weeks in a month, and twelve months in a year.

1197. In a village in Groningen, the Netherlands, there is a large fort in the shape of a star. It was built in 1593 with the intention to control the only road between Germany and the city of Groningen, which was controlled by the Spaniards during the time of the Eighty Years War.
1198. Phoenix Jones was a martial artist who led a superhero movement in Seattle that was actually pretty successful. The group prevented several assaults and robberies until 2014.
1199. The United Kingdom has a right to roam, which allows public access for walking in leisure to spots like mountains, moors, heaths, and downs that are privately owned.
1200. In November of 2016, a strong earthquake with a 7.8 magnitude tore through New Zealand. It was so powerful that it actually dragged the sea floor 6.6 feet (two meters) above ground. In fact, it was still crawling in sea life when it was discovered.

AFTERWORD

Did you enjoy the book or learn something new? It really helps out small publishers like Scott Matthews if you could leave a quick review on Amazon so others in the community can also find the book!

⭐ ⭐ ⭐ ⭐ ⭐